The Golden Legions Of Hope

by
Nan C. Cataldi

The Golden Legions Of Hope

BOOK 3
OF
THE KEYS OF BEING TRILOGY

by
Nan C. Cataldi

Cover Illustration by Mark Sean Wilson

INKWELL BOOKS
Writing-Publishing-Printing

Nan C. Cataldi

ISBN: 978-0-9728118-0-4
Library of Congress Control Number: 2019946195

Published by Inkwell Books LLC
10632 North Scottsdale Road, Unit 695
Scottsdale, AZ 85254
Tel. 480-315-3781
E-mail info@inkwellbooksllc.com
Website www.inkwellbooksllc.com

INKWELL BOOKS
Writing · Publishing · Printing

DEDICATION

This book is dedicated to all the plant and animal species that have lost their lives in the burning fires of the Amazon Rainforest.

The Golden Legions of Hope

Table of Contents

The Golden Legions of Hope

CHAPTER 1

JOURNEY TO THE ALTAR

As the Earth's environment was getting worse, so were the mounting attacks by the Dark Ones on the Fae-rens. The Planet's imbalance increased the evil's power more, since it thrived on it. The Cursed One knew the Protector Fae-rens would appear anywhere animals were in danger. In all the millennia the Fae-rens had lived, none had ever lost their life, until their leader Phan-non was captured, and his life was ended by three of Hitler's most evil sorcerers in 1941. Now almost weekly, three or four Fae-rens were losing his or her life to Fellon the Cursed's sorcerers.

As Glymirra, the half eagle, half human-like ruler of the magical world of Wren, began her journey to the Altar of Hope, she received a message of distress from a group of Protector Fae-rens on Gaeya. Her spirit creatures in the northern part of Gaeya were being attacked by two powerful sorcerers, who were accompanied by several enchanted wolves. Two of the

Fae-rens had changed their forms into Elks, which made them more vulnerable to the attacks. Even transformed, their aura of goodness could be felt by some of the more powerful sorcerers.

This attack happened while the Fae-rens were moving more than two hundred elk and some smaller endangered animals to safety from a volcanic eruption. The volcano, which had been dormant for thousands of years, had begun spewing ashes all over the lower countryside of western Canada without warning.

Upon receiving the urgent message, Glymirra contacted Kendar, the white-winged centaur, who was given charge of Wren in her absence. He was to immediately dispatch five Sentinels and ten more Protector Fae-rens to assist them. She had to stay on her course; she must hasten the repair of Gaeya, which was becoming increasingly unstable from all the catastrophic events destroying the land. The lives of all Gaeya's creations rested in her hands.

The Grand One continued her flight to unite the four Keys of Being, which would restore balance to Gaeya and disrupt the evil taking over the land. Recently the Grand One had received the lost Elka, the fourth Key of Being, from the young human Guardian, Nicky Kirkland. She and her guard of Fae-rens were traveling to the Grotto deep inside Gaeya to place them in the crystal Altar of Hope to begin the healing of the Earth.

In the meantime, Kendar, and his centaur guards would protect the four gates into Wren, which aligned themselves to the four doorways that change as the Earth rotates. These portals could only be accessed by mortal Guardians entering Wren. Every six hours, in a different part of the planet, a portal can be opened with the use of an opulan, a gold disk given to a Guardian so they may enter the outer perimeter of Wren. Worldwide, there are forty-eight portals; each can be open for a peri-arten or thirty mortal minutes. Every three days the same one is available for a Guardian to enter. This knowledge is only known by the Grand Glymirra, so that the invisible veil to Wren remains protected from any evil that may try to enter the peaceful realm.

CHAPTER 2

FELLON'S FORTRESS

While Glymirra was traveling to the Grotto to reset the balance to Gaeya, the dark sorcerers, Shredd and Tarr, arrived at an ancient fortress built into one of the Himalayan mountains. They carried with them two Fae-ren prisoners they had captured in the desert while chasing the human Guardian, who had possessed the gold disk and the Elka.

Shredd, who had sweat dripping down his face, was anxious to report to his master, Fellon. He hoped that the delivery of the gold disk would keep the Dark One's mind off the Elka, the last Key of Being, which Shredd had lost when the teenage Guardian disappeared during the mine cave-in caused by a violent earthquake. He was buried under a huge pile of rocks and debris. All that remained was his denim cap and the gold disk. He was sure Fellon the Cursed did not know he had a chance to possess the Key, and he did not want to be the one to tell the sinister sorcerer that it was gone.

"Tarr, take the prisoners to the dungeon. I will talk to the Cursed One and give him the gold object he has been searching for. And I will let him know the boy died in the mine cave-in during the earthquake. I have his blue cap for proof."

Tarr descended to the lowest level of the dark, damp fortress, which had been used hundreds of years ago as a prison for those who had deposed the local emperor. As he walked, floating behind the sorcerer in an invisible cage were the Fae-rens Brin-dah and Der-rex, still laying in an unconscious state from the lightening– like spells shot at them while protecting their Guardian. When the ebony shrouded sorcerer reached the bottom, he waved his hand over a small wall torch, which lit instantly.

As he continued to make his way down the cold and gloomy, narrow corridor, the already hunched-back sorcerer had to stoop further to prevent hitting the low stone ceiling, which slowed his progress. Finally, Tarr reached the last tiny cell at the end of the passage. The thick, heavy, wooden door into this cell was ajar. The sorcerer opened the door further and with a swish of his finger, the cage with the transformed Fae-rens flew into the cell, hitting the back wall, then sliding down to rest on the dirt floor. Waving his hand, he whispered a dark spell then used his magic finger to slam the heavy door closed, causing dust and debris to billow all around the ancient door. This made the sorcerer cough. Then he smiled wickedly to himself. Tarr was curious to return to the main level of the fortress to find out if the Cursed One would reward him. So, he turned his back to the cell, became a flame of bright red and disappeared.

Shredd appeared in a flash in front of the large door of the fortress tower. Inside was the most evil of all sorcerers, Fellon the Cursed. He sat on a large stone throne worn by time, contemplating his next moves on Gaeya and Wren.

Outside the door Shredd hesitated, fearing that the Cursed One might not be happy with his news. Fellon wanted the Elka, the Lost Key of Being, but he only had the gold disk. Beads of sweat now dripped off his brow as he slowly opened the door.

Hearing the creak of the heavy door, immediately Fellon stood up. In a deep, raspy voice, he said, "Shredd, I have been waiting for your return. Do you have it?"

"I...I have the gold object you seek, Cursed One."

"Excellent, Shredd." An evil grin formed on the dark face of Fellon. *Now that I have the opulan. I can enter a portal into Wren,* he thought.

When Shredd heard this praise, he relaxed a little.

"Where is the boy? He will know how and where to use it."

Strained and agitated again, the tired sorcerer responded nervously, "The boy is dead. He was killed in the mine shaft when an earthquake hit. He was buried under several tons of rubble. All that could be retrieved was the gold disk and the boy's blue cap."

Shredd reached into the pocket of his black robe and pulled out the blue denim cap and the gold disk. He was alarmed to see that the gold disk that had been open when he put it in his robe was now closed. Without words, he opened his hand to show the opulan to Fellon.

But Fellon saw the look on Shredd's face. "What is wrong?" he screamed in a roaring voice. The entire room shook, and dust filled the air.

Afraid to speak, Shredd cowered down in confusion, very upset.

"I hear your thoughts. The gold disk is not open, as you found it."

Fellon grabbed the disk from Shredd and tried to pry it open. It had become solid. No cracks existed anywhere on it. *But how is that possible?*

"Glymirra is more clever than I thought," he laughed half-heartedly.

Shredd was mildly relieved and began to tell Fellon that the gold disk had been open in two halves. Inside he had seen an arm with bird's wings, like a pointer. Then he told the Cursed One they had captured two Fae-rens that were with the boy, and Tarr had taken them to the dungeon below.

This information excited Fellon even more. *Without the boy, they would know where to find the Key of Being and give him the locations of some of the portals into Wren. Invasion was imminent!*

At this very moment, he had sent several of his more powerful sorcerers to capture and put a very potent spell on the North Wind twins. The twins were the strongest of all the winds. Since the Fae-rens used the winds to help them travel to different destinations, this move would greatly hinder them. Also, the bitter cold they send would slow their rescues. The spirit creatures would be unable to aid many of the animals struggling to survive the increasing cataclysmic dangers on Earth. This capture would definitely put the Fae-rens at a disadvantage and ensure the evil's victory over Gaeya, helping with the invasion of the world of Wren. All was going well for Fellon and his sorcerers at this time.

CHAPTER 3

FAE-REN PRISONERS

The sudden smashing of the cage against the stone wall woke both Fae-rens as they began returning from animal and human forms to their invisible Fae-ren forms. Their eyes were trying to focus and assess the surroundings. Der-rex spoke first, "Where are we? The last thing I remember was fighting the sorcerers in the desert." His face flushed in horror, "Oh, no! I hope Nicky made it to Wren with the Elka."

Brin-dah shook her head to clear the foggy feeling, *I must remember what happened.* The Fae-ren sat with her eyes closed, concentrating on what could have happened. But after a few minutes, she, too, could only remember battling the sorcerers in the desert. Brin-dah looked around the freezing cold, small, dank, stone room. "I think we are in a very old dungeon. But how did we get here, and where is here?"

With a concerned look on his face, Der-rex responded, "We must be the prisoners of the Cursed One. I only hope Say-den and Brem-mer made it back to Wren safe. During our encounter with the sorcerers, I thought I saw Say-den get hit by a bolt of lightning from that sorcerer, who seemed to appear out of nowhere."

"Der-rex, if we are the prisoners of Fellon, why would he keep us alive?"

"I do not know. Unless...he thinks we can help him breach the Veil into Wren," he responded, looking very troubled.

Brin-dah, distressed by the thought of being taken to Fellon, spouted, "We have to find a way to get out of here and fast!"

Der-rex slowly moved around the small cage, assessing their predicament. After a moment he looked at Brin-dah and asked, "Do you think we can contact the Grand One or are the walls too thick for our telepathy?"

"I will try, but first we need to get out of this cage." Brin-dah answered. Der-rex. "Let us hold hands to see if we are strong enough to break through these bars."

The two Fae-rens joined hands to increase their magical powers and began to concentrate on freedom. The two began chanting in a low but strong voice "Dissa, dissa, dissa..." The chanting grew louder and louder. The spirit creatures concentrated with all their might. The invisible cage began to vibrate violently. Then it burst apart, liberating Brin-dah and Der-rex. Excited and relieved, they embraced one another for a moment.

Brin-dah smiled at Der-rex. "Now I will send a message to the Grand One." She closed her eyes, then touched her finger to her forehead. With her mind focused on Wren, she tried to send a telepathic message for help. But she felt a force push back on her, nearly knocking her down. She tried once again to send a message and this time was thrown to the floor by an unseen energy.

" 'Tis a kind of barrier preventing me from contacting Wren. We must find a way to get out of here. If we can escape this cell, I may be able to contact Wren for help."

"I agree." Der-rex replied, "But we must hurry. I fear the Cursed One or one of his sorcerers will show-up here soon to question or torture us."

Neither one had any idea how long they had been there. The two walked around the small cell looking for a way to escape. Both checked the dirt floor and the stone ceiling. They discovered the cell was protected by enchantments stronger than their Fae-ren magic. They kept turning around and around the mini cell, looking and thinking of some way to escape.

Brin-dah began staring at the very small niche which was inserted into the upper part of the door about one foot from the top. It was covered by a small wooden panel. Brin-dah pointed to the wee door. Der-rex looked up and smiled. *Maybe the niche was a weak point that they could open with their combined magic.*

Der-rex, hearing her thoughts, agreed they should combine their powers to remove the small wooden cover hiding the tiny window and escape through it. Somehow, they had to get a message out to Glymirra.

CHAPTER 4

GUARDIAN ENLIGHTENED

In the outer perimeter of mystical Wren, Nicky Kirkland stood surveying the beautiful place he had entered through the magical portal. The teen saw many, many fields of multi-colored flowers, and in the distance a mystical solid rainbow hung in the sky. Rows of large trees could be seen ahead as he walked along the cobblestone pathway. This calm, serene place helped the teen to relax and nearly forget the dangers he had encountered on his journey to the portal. As he moved forward, Nicky became more and more in awe of the outer realm of Wren.

He noticed groups of deer, elk, and other smaller mammals gathering at the farthest point of the outer realm. As he stopped to ponder why the animals were gathered there, the teen's stomach began to growl. He suddenly realized how weak and exhausted he had become from his quest to return the fourth Key of Being to Glymirra.

Nicky began to look around for Kendar's return. He was to bring the young Guardian some much-needed nourishment. Spending three days in the desert being pursued by evil sorcerers and running on adrenaline, with no water or food except for one day's worth of his school lunch, took its toll!

A few minutes later Kendar appeared with food and drink. He handed Nicky a gold plate filled with strange green and purple slices of fruit and a silver chalice with lemon-smelling liquid. Trying not to be rude, Nicky took the plate, hesitated for a brief moment, then tasted a piece of the purple fruit.

"Wow! This is delicious," Nicky said in surprise. Famished, he ate greedily, shoving the food in his mouth, barely even chewing. He finished the plate then handed it back to Kendar. The Guardian took the chalice and drained the tasty lemon drink. Feeling energized and super relaxed, he thanked Kendar.

"Is this the fruit the Fae-rens eat?"

"Yes, Guardian. This is what all inhabitants of Wren eat. This fruit is why all the animals and Fae-rens of Wren live in harmony together and do not grow old and die."

Blown away by the enlightening information, Nicky swallowed and tried to imagine a world of everlasting life.

Feeling a little uncomfortable he paused and looked around, again watching the groups of animals at the edge of the orchards close to what looked like the outer edge of Wren. Hoping to understand what was happening, he asked the centaur, "Why are those animals huddled into groups over there?"

"You do realize the number of forest fires burning, volcanoes erupting, and floods happening on Gaeya - your Earth."

"Well, yeah. It's...scary!" Nicky said shivering.

"Well, the Protector Fae-rens will bring animals behind the Veil when they are in extreme danger and unable to move them to a safe area near their homes. Once the danger lessens, the animals are returned to their homes. That is why the Fae-rens were created. They protect and serve all life on Gaeya. Although they are not to directly interfere in human affairs. Right now, there are a lot of animals that cannot go home, so they are staying here until it's safe."

Once again surprised, Nicky responded, "Wow, it is difficult to realize someone magical has always been helping our planet survive. It is totally amazing. I vaguely remember Brin-dah and Der-rex telling me this five years ago. But it didn't register to me at the time."

Kendar waved a hand, saying, "Please make yourself comfortable under one of the trees ahead or have a seat on a marble bench. I am awaiting information regarding the opulan you dropped outside of Wren just as you entered the portal, I am sure our Grand Glymirra will be..."

But Kendar stopped in mid-sentence. His eyes widened and his face looked strained. He had just received a disturbing message. He abruptly turned and galloped toward the doorway through which Nicky had entered several minutes before.

Shocked by Kendar's behavior, Nicky started to run after the centaur. As the teen grew closer to him, Kendar raised his staff, and Nicky halted.

"Go Back! I must secure Wren."

For the first time, since he entered Wren, Nicky was terrified. *What was going on?* He started walking back down the cobblestone path toward the distant trees, stopping every few minutes to look for Kendar. But the majestic Centaur had vanished.

CHAPTER 5

RETURN TO WREN

Meanwhile, a hundred and one Fae-ren Protectors moved with the swift wind, acting as an escort for their leader, Glymirra, the Keeper of the Balance. Cloaked in an invisible form, she was hurrying to the Secret Grotto deep below the Earth's crust. The ruler of Wren carried on her the four Keys of Being. It was imperative that she get to the Grotto, descend to the Altar of Hope and place the Keys into the mystical, triangular crystal, thus restoring balance to the planet. The escalating chaotic weather, volcanic eruptions and earthquakes were beginning to tear Gaeya apart. All life forms were in danger. Returning the Keys to their proper place would enable Gaeya to heal at a very fast rate and decrease the control of the Evil Ones.

Fellon the Cursed and his cronies were gaining increased dark powers over many of the living, not realizing they would soon have no one to control, as soon as the balance was returned.

The Grand one had been in flight for only a minute or two

when she received an urgent telepathic message from Kendar the centaur, whom she had left in charge of the world of Wren in her absence. *The opulan, the gold disk that opened the portal to Wren for the Guardian Nicky Kirkland was taken by an evil entity. All are on alert in Wren.*

Shocked by the message, Glymirra halted in mid-air. She responded immediately, transmitting her message silently to Kendar. *Close all the entrances and portals into Wren at once! The Altar will have to wait. I am on my way back. We must prepare immediately for the Evil's attack!*

No sooner had she replied to Kendar's message when she received an emergency message from the North Wind. His twin brother had been put under a strong enchantment by several of Fellon's sorcerers. Now controlled by the evil, the twin was sending strong, frigid winds to tropical areas, confusing not only the animals there, but also the humans. The intense cold sent many animals into early hibernation and others to seek shelter.

Upon hearing this news, she sent a telepathic message to the Fae-rens guarding her travel route to return at once to Wren. Confused by the Grand One's message, all halted in mid-air briefly and the hundred and one Protectors immediately began to head back to the mystical realm.

Glymirra arrived ahead of the Protector Fae-rens. She landed in front of her stone and marble palace sanctuary still in her invisible form. In the blink of an eye, the ruler appeared in her solid form, startling her pterodactyl guard. Glymirra addressed him. "Send for the remainder of my Protectors to return home at once! Please have them stand in squad formation here. I will be back soon to address them."

Shocked by the order from his normally serene master, the pterodactyl sent a telepathic message to all the Protector Fae-rens: *Our Grand One demands all Protectors must immediately report to Wren and form units at the front of the palace sanctuary.*

Several thousand Protectors were helping animals and sea creatures cope with the disasters happening to their habitats, hiding and moving them to safety. When they received this strange message, many Fae-rens became alarmed. They quickly secured the animals they were aiding, and headed for Wren, realizing the Grand One would not summon them unless it was of extreme importance. After all, they were at war with the Evil Fellon. Touching the magical orbs around their necks and catching a ride on the winds, they began arriving in Wren by the hundreds.

Glymirra hurried into her quarters in the rear of the palace. She approached the large round, shimmering blue crystal that hung on her wall. The Grand One asked to see Fellon whereabouts, but the Reflection of Ages just clouded over with no results. Frustrated, she thought, *his evil powers are still too strong. He is shielding me from the truth.*

She left the mystical crystal and now approached the huge, egg-shaped gold object that rested in the corner of the room. With a wave of her hand, the gold object shook mightily and then began to open. She reached inside and pulled out an ancient manuscript. The words were in a strange language that only the Grand One could read. The magical book bore the name "The Powerous: Book of Extreme Incantations." Each page was written on paper-thin gold leaves. In all the thousands of years she had nurtured Gaeya, she had never needed to use the ultimate magic spoken within this book. But she had no choice. As mighty as Glymirra's supernatural powers were, she could no longer defeat the very strong evil all alone. She would have to use the "Powerous."

Her special Protector Fae-rens were not created to fight

like soldiers. They were given magic only to protect. That is why after thousands of years of their existence, they were now being destroyed by the evil sorcerers. Many of the animals they were helping had also succumbed to the wicked, without the protection of the Fae-rens.

It was not openly known, but since the rise of the present evil, which had started in 1941, more than four thousand Protectors had lost their lives, adding to Glymirra's decision. Before that time no Fae-ren had ever lost their lives. Five or six thousand years ago it was thought that if a Fae-ren entered a mortal dwelling they would lose their powers or turn to stone. But Glymirra herself told them that story to keep her Fae-rens from interfering with mortals. It was against the supernatural code to bother any mortals, and all spirit creatures must obey.

CHAPTER 6

THE JEWELED GATE

Nicky caught a glimpse of Kendar and some of the other centaurs moving swiftly toward the beautiful gold and jeweled gate, which is the entrance to inner Wren. He had to know what was going on and when he would be able to return home to check on his mother and his friends. So, he ran after them. He was fast on the football field, but the teen could not catch up to the them. After all, they had the lower body and legs of a horse.

Nevertheless, Nicky continued to race toward the gate. In the distance, he saw the huge, sparkling, golden gate open then close quickly. The beautiful rainbow he saw earlier in the distance, began to dissipate. All that remained in front of him were the fields of flowers and rows of fruit trees that lined the cobblestone path. Suddenly, he was alone.

He decided to continue down the path toward the large, brilliantly shiny gateway. He needed to figure out a way to enter the inner realm of this magical world. But no mortal had ever entered this secret world. Not even a Guardian. Drawing closer to the golden gate, he suddenly stopped.

Nicky now embraced the sight of the breathtaking gate. It was sixty feet tall and forty feet wide with blue, red, white, and purple crystal gems embedded on and all around the golden frame. It was mesmerizing. They gave off a mystical light so strong the teen had to squint to appreciate it.

He shook his head as if in a dream then moved closer. As he arrived within two yards of the gate, he heard thundering hooves approaching. He threw himself behind a large tree loaded with purple and green fruit. Peeking around, he saw a small group of centaurs galloping at great speed. In no time the gigantic gate began to open. Nicky knew this may be his only chance to gain entrance. He just had to follow the five centaurs through the great gate. He hoped he could enter unnoticed with all the scurrying he saw going on ahead of him.

Nicky sucked in a deep breath and ran in behind them. As soon as he entered, he stopped abruptly, and his mouth dropped open in awe. The teen did not expect to see such a sight. Animals and birds he only read about but had never seen, not even in a zoo, were rushing around in a disoriented manner: small and large dinosaurs, mammoths and mastodons, huge eagles and prehistoric birds, dragon–like creatures, strange tigers, bears that only walked upright–all were running or flying about.

Then he realized he could see the Fae-rens. *But they were invisible to humans. How was he able to see them now?* They looked almost human but had small hands and tiny feet. They stood about four feet tall and wore green and white knee-length tunics. Short red hair covered their heads.

Amazed and surprised by the vision before him, he almost forgot he did not belong here. No human was permitted into this realm. Suddenly he felt eyes staring at him. A small, gray dinosaur with a long neck spotted him. He knew he had to find cover before he was discovered by the Fae-rens or a centaur. Nicky looked around in horror, then ducked behind a large bush near the gate he had just entered. He expected an alarm to go off by his human presence. But as the small dinosaur looked around again, he saw no one.

Red-faced with his heart racing, the teen watched from his hiding place. He needed to find out why all of Wren seemed terrified. The teen had to know what had happened in the last few minutes. He feared for his family on Earth even though

Glymirra assured him they were well protected not only by the Sentinels but by magic.

Nicky waited in hiding, watching as the unique animals and birds living there were being rounded up by the worker Fae-rens. As he silently watched, groups of Fae-rens with wing-like arms, slightly larger than the workers, appeared out of nowhere and began gliding toward the palace sanctuary. Curious, he started to move closer toward the commotion, trying not to be detected. All the chaos helped. He sought out large trees and large rock formations to hide behind as he slowly made his way further into the interior of Wren.

Nicky was again in awe of all the strange animals and birds he saw. He passed very close to a mastodon, then a unicorn. The unicorn was smaller than he had imagined; only about the size of a German Shepard. Still no human had ever, ever laid eyes on some of these prehistoric animals and creatures of myth. For a moment he forgot he was afraid and felt fortunate instead.

Nicky's curiosity pushed him even closer to Glymirra's Palace. He knew he must move at a cautious pace, again darting behind trees and brush as he progressed further, so as not to be discovered. The scene in front of him was beginning to get overwhelming. He rubbed his eyes again, unable to grasp such a spectacle, as thousands of Protectors began appearing above him as they continued to glide into the realm. Each of them landed in front of the marble palace he spied ahead.

Looking to his left, Nicky watched as the animal inhabitants were herded into groups and moved away by worker Fae-rens to shelters located several hundred yards from the Palace. He waited and watched as the several thousand Protector Fae-rens lined up to form units. It was like a human military formation before a parade. In a single long line on the left were fifty Centaurs. Next to them, also in a single long line, stood fifty gray hawk Sentinels. The only inhabitants of Wren that were not here were the few Sentinels protecting Nicky's family and friends.

Nicky remained hidden, watching with intense curiosity. The sight of the magnitude of the formations was very worrisome. *Something very devastating must have happened. Could the great evil enter Wren or take over the Earth? Was the opulan he lost somehow connected to this disturbing sight?* These thoughts began to haunt him. *Could he be somehow be responsible for all this pandemonium?*

Agitated, he decided to creep even closer. Crouching down he moved very slowly forward, again hiding behind any bush, tree, boulder or marble bench he encountered. Nicky was within twenty feet of the Fae-rens' frontline when he realized there was nothing ahead to hide behind. He had to stay hidden behind the giant bush where he now knelt, waiting. It felt like something of great importance must be about to happen. *I hope my Mom and Molly are okay.* He was overcome by the enormous vision before him. It was so scary. He trembled as he awaited the outcome of this scene.

CHAPTER 7

THE POWEROUS

As the Fae-rens continued to assemble, Glymirra read over the incantation required to transform her Protector Fae-rens into magical super soldiers, capable of powers equal to or greater than Fellon's sorcerers. The evil was winning, so the Grand One needed to even the odds. No one on Gaeya or Wren could understand the ancient language spoken to perform this powerful spell. Only the ruler of Wren, sent from the Universe, would know.

The Grand One walked over to a marble perch, which held her royal cloak. In preparation for performing the incantation she took the royal blue cape and placed it over her feathered shoulders. She paced around her chambers nervously, awaiting all the Protector Fae-rens.

The Fae-ren Legions would not be able to change their appearance while under the mighty enchantment of The Powerous, but the spell would increase their magic, making them much more powerful than a regular Protector. Also, they would be given armor protection and the skills of great soldiers.

Even though the incantation was originally only for the Fae-rens, Glymirra knew they also needed powers to protect the world of Wren. The Centaurs and the gray, hawk Sentinels would become more powerful than normal. While most of the transformed Fae-rens would be on Gaeya fighting and protecting all the living there, a few would remain to assist the Centaurs, protecting the doorways into Wren. Others would be sent to help the humans with the mounting disasters caused by the Earth's imbalance and by the Evil Fellon. In their new forms with increased powers, this would be easier.

Just as the great ruler of Wren was about to leave her chambers to address the creatures gathered in front of her palace, she received an emergency message from the captured Brin-dah, alerting her of the Fae-rens recent attempted to escape from Fellon's lair. "Where are they?" she whispered to herself. *I cannot help them until the Keys of Being are returned to the Altar of Hope. I must save both worlds now! It is the only way.*

Glymirra hurried out of the palace, appearing at the front carrying the golden "Powerous: Book of Extreme Incantations" in her hands. She paused, her face showing deep concern as she looked over the more than forty thousand Fae-ren Protectors standing before her. This was the first time since the beginning of Wren that all Protectors were assembled together. They stood poised and silent. It was an awesome sight.

The Grand One whispered, and a marble lectern magically appeared. She placed the heavy book on it. The whole of Wren was in total silence. Even the Workers attending the animal inhabitants were overcome by the site of all the Protectors, Centaurs and Sentinels. They, too, stood paused in anticipation of Glymirra's address. Once again, she looked over the Protectors of her realm.

The silence was almost disturbing. It made this beautiful, calm place now seem oppressive and eerie. The feeling caused Nicky to shiver. But the curious teen remained hidden in a squatted position, waiting for the Ruler of the Realm to speak. He hoped he would be able to comprehend her language. After all, since he had entered this magical world, the teen could now see the Fae-rens that were invisible to him on Earth. Maybe the magic within this place would help him to understand the words.

Glymirra began to speak, "We are all in grave danger at this time. The evil Fellon now possesses an opulan to open a portal into Wren. I received a message only seconds ago that two of my most trusted Protectors are being held prisoners by him. I was also contacted by the North Wind, informing me his Twin brother was kidnapped by sorcerers and put under a strong spell. He is now freezing tropical areas of Gaeya so that Fellon can control them and all the living within those areas.

"As you can see, our entire existence is threatened, and extreme measures must be taken to ensure the balance is restored and the evil weakened. So, today, I will use extreme supernatural powers to see you are given every advantage to carry out the mission of saving our two worlds.

"You, my Protector Fae-rens, have been very faithful in guarding and caring for the living on Gaeya for many millennia. But you are not soldiers. We are up against a force more evil than ever before. This is the first time since your existence that we have lost Protectors. More than four thousand of you have perished already from confrontation with Fellon's Dark Ones. All of you are having more and more difficulty taking care of the animals on Gaeya because of the interference from the evil sorcerers. When we lose one of our Protectors to evil, the balance is further upset, causing the evil to grow stronger.'"

As the thousands of Fae-ren, Sentinels, and Centaurs stoically listened to the speech, Nicky stayed hidden. He was excited at the fact he understood everything said by Glymirra. But he was also worried by what she said. He, too, remained focused on the Grand One's every word.

"I have consulted the ancient 'Powerous.' The words on its pages will increase your powers and transform you into high-level soldiers. You will be capable of matching or exceeding the powers of any sorcerer of Fellon the Cursed, except for maybe the Evil One himself.

"Fae-rens, you will have the ability to stop the evil, but you will not be able to change your form. Most of the living on Gaeya will still be able to see or sense you. Only the mortals will not know you are there.

"Sentinels, your strength will increase by two times. This will also be true for all the Centaurs.

"Now, I ask you to continue to stand quietly, as I begin the incantation. I will then instruct you on your assignments afterwards."

Adjusting the robe around her shoulders, the Grand One looked down and opened the 'Powerous' manuscript before her. She nodded to her Legions. Then as her mouth began to move, an eerie sound could be heard by all. The incantation was not in words, but in a melodical type of music. The eerie sound became a low- pitched, strange, calming hum. Then all of a sudden, gold crystal flakes began to fall like snow from above. The flakes began to cover the Fae-ren Legions and all the others standing in formation.

Listening to the strange, peaceful musical sounds, Nicky stood up in a trance-like state, forgetting where he was. The teen began receiving the flecks of gold which covered his body from head to toe. He soon realized what he had done but was unable to move. He was completely frozen in place. He could see Glymirra's mouth moving as the humming sound began to slow. *Now what was he to do? He was not supposed to be there. What would happen to him when the music stopped, and he was discovered?*

The musical sound slowed then stopped. A bright illumination began to grow around everyone covered with the golden snow.

Nicky could feel a weird tingling begin from his head and extend down his entire body to his feet. He was terrified by this sensation. Panicking he tried to struggle but remained unable to move a single muscle. *Help! What is happening to me?!*

The illumination became a huge fiery ball, then exploded in a flash. *Boom!* As the bright light dimmed, Glymirra stood admiring her supernatural accomplishment. The Grand One's Protector Fae-rens now appeared as amazing superior soldiers. The Legions of Wren were clad in gold breast plates, helmets, shields and golden shimmering swords. Eagle's wings erupted from behind their shoulders.

Suddenly her eyes focused on a strange sight never seen before in the inner realm. It was the young Guardian, Nicky Kirkland. He was taller, more muscular, also dressed like a soldier, including huge wings. But how did he get here unnoticed? Glymirra was baffled at first, then a large smile spread across her face.

Nicky was in shock. He felt the weight of the wings and gold breast plate with the accessories. Then the teen saw the special soldiers in front of him, realizing he looked similar and thought, *Whoa! Look at me.* He whispered "Awesome!"

Next, he felt the Ruler of Wren watching him. At first, the teen was fearful. He wasn't sure he would be accepted here. But the grinning Glymirra nodded favorably. He relaxed for a minute but soon became very excited. The teen felt so special.

This time he would be able to fight the evil, not only with his wit or the help of the Key of Being, but with supernatural powers of his own given to him by the powerful incantation spoken by Glymirra.

Glymirra, pleased by the spell's outcome, viewed her soldiers. Soon they would be dispatched to all areas of Gaeya to protect, once again. Now the two worlds had hope! The magical transformation gave the Protectors a chance against Fellon and his Dark Ones.

"Now you have the knowledge and strength to thwart the evil sorcerers you will encounter. Use your swords to weaken the dark ones. It will halt them from advancing and bind them if needed. Do not destroy them, if possible. Once I have returned the Keys of Being to the Altar of Hope, most of the Evil Ones will lose a large portion of their powers.

"But be aware. Your auras are also stronger. It will be easier for the evil to feel you or maybe even see a faint outline of you. Protect yourself and the others in need.

"I want my Fae-rens that were helping those on Gaeya to return to your charges. One group of you will search for and rescue the spellbound North Wind, captured by Fellon's cronies. I will search the Reflection of Ages to give you the Wind's precise location and how many captors are guarding him. You will leave with the rest of the Protectors, and I will send you a message with your destination and number of sorcerers you will be facing.

"Except for a few Sentinels that will accompany me, the remaining hawks and Centaurs will protect the four entrances into our realm. Ten Protector Fae-rens will remain here to assist the Centaurs and Sentinels in guarding the four doorways into Wren and safeguarding the inhabitants of our realm. I would like our Guardian Nicky, to help rescue Brin-dah and Der-rex, who are being held by the Evil Fellon."

Surprised by the teen's presence in the inner part of this realm, all turned at once to look at him. Nicky squirmed a little, feeling uncomfortable by thousands of stares. Then he saw many, many smiles from the Legions. The teen immediately relaxed.

"Nicky, you will be sent to free Brin-dah and Der-rex, once I locate their whereabouts. I will send one of my Protectors with you, Brem-mer. He helped you in the desert where he lost his mate Say-den from a sorcerer's attack. I will join you once the Keys are reunited."

The Grand One scanned her warrior Legions. With a wave

of her hand, they all began to leave formation to begin their journeys to Gaeya.

"Kendar, you will oversee all in Wren while I return the Keys of Being to the Altar, restoring the balance to Gaeya. Then I will join our Guardian and Brem-mer in rounding up the evil sorcerers. Now go!"

CHAPTER 8

THE REFLECTION OF AGES

Taking a deep breath, Glymirra turned abruptly and entered her palace. Nicky and Brem-mer stood outside awaiting her return. The Grand One hurried over to consult the Reflection of Ages. The blue sapphire crystal was glowing brighter than ever before. Had the spell increased its powers, too?

"First, show me where the Evil is holding the twin of the North Wind, so I may determine how many of my new soldiers I need to send to its rescue."

The great Reflection of Ages hazed over and quickly located the whereabouts of the North Wind. He was being held on a small island off the coast of Antarctica. As the Grand One surveyed the area, she counted seventy-one dark- hooded sorcerers guarding a large cave. It was imperative to return the North Wind's Twin to his proper place and halt the evil freeze to the tropics. She sent the message to one of her Protector Fae-rens, who would lead 100 others in the rescue. With this telepathic message received from their leader, the Protector soldiers touched their newly energized orbs and began their swift journey to Antarctica.

Glymirra closed her eyes and waved her hand over the huge, blue crystal once more. It glowed even brighter. Then concentrating harder than ever before, she thought, *I need to know all I can about Fellon the Cursed. Show me how he evolved into this powerful sorcerer. Then show me where he is holding Brin-dah and Der-rex.*

The great Reflection of Ages hazed over once more. In a few seconds the crystal cleared. The year 1941 briefly flashed before the scene, which showed a German soldier standing guard outside an encampment as a jeep pulled up with three strange-looking black cloaked figures. Their faces were hidden by large hoods. The three mysterious, dark men stepped out of the vehicle and began walking toward the opening of the gate. The soldier watched silently as they passed him, the aura of a Fae-ren faintly shining around him. In an instant, the last figure reeled around, lifted his arm and sent a bolt of lightning out of his fingers, striking the soldier in his chest. He was immediately frozen in place.

Glymirra now knew that that the soldier was a transformed Fae-ren. In fact, it was Phan-non, the former leader of the

Fae-rens. As Fae-rens are more vulnerable when they transform from their spirit form to another living form, the Grand One watched with attentiveness, trying to understand how he was captured and ultimately destroyed.

The crystal flashed again. Next, she saw the Fae-ren soldier chained between two large trees. The evil sorcerers were walking around him, chanting curses at him and casting powerful spells. The hunched-back sorcerer, whose lightning bolt had paralyzed Phan-non, approached him, carrying a large goblet in the shape of a skull. He forced a dark, thick liquid down the trapped Fae-ren's throat. His aura began flickering and eventually, it turned black. Glymirra's Fae-ren was dead. She felt saddened once more.

The sorcerers continued cursing the body of Phan-non. This ritual lasted for several hours. When the hunched sorcerer, the most powerful of them, raised his blackened arm, all three sorcerers together began chanting. Then all three raised their arms, sending a combined lightning bolt at the lifeless Fae-ren. The body of Phan-non jerked. It was very eerie to see her deceased Fae-ren move.

Glymirra continued to watch with great grief and curiosity. Again, a sorcerer approached the limp body with the goblet filled with a boiling, red potion. The figure roughly lifted Phan-non's head and poured the bubbling liquid into his open mouth. Once more, the three evil ones sent a combined lightning bolt at the Fae-ren's chest. The body jumped and jerked several more times. Then, the drooping head moved. It slowly raised up. Shocked at the sight, Glymirra shivered to see an empty-eyed Phan-non move. The sorcerers celebrated as they marveled at their new brother. They had been successful. They untied him, lifting him to his feet. He stood expressionless, as if awaiting orders. The most evil of the three, walked over to him. "I see you have great inner power. We have cursed you, turning you into one of us. But I will teach you, and you will become a very powerful sorcerer!" Then the Dark One raised his arms up and shot lightning into the sky, crowing with his success.

The Reflection of Ages misted over once more. As it began to clear, the year 1987 appeared very briefly. Then it showed two dark figures. One very hunched over, covered by a long, tattered, black cloak. The other standing erect with a long, very shiny black cloak. The two seemed to be battling each other. Their arms were raised, and lightning bolts flew out of their fingers, back-and-forth as each one ducked to avoid being struck. Finally, the tattered and hunched dark sorcerer was hit in the chest by one bolt then another, collapsing to the ground, unmoving. It was over. The other sorcerer lifted both arms into the air, shouting, "I am the most powerful sorcerer of all time! I am Fellon the Cursed!" The crystal faded.

Glymirra was very disturbed by what she saw and realized her former leader of the Fae-rens was now her most powerful enemy. Now she knew how the evil was so knowledgeable about Fae-ren habits. She began to gather her thoughts and proceed as planned. This evil takeover must be stopped now!

Suddenly, the Reflection of Ages misted over again, then rapidly cleared, revealing an old fortress carved into the rock high in the Himalayan Mountain range. She waved her hand over the site to get an in-depth view of the layout and anyone within. It showed three floors and a high tower with a dungeon deep in the center. There were three thousand or more occupants inside and out. Many large animals and hooded figures moved about the floors, some entering and leaving by magic.

In the high tower an almost-human shape appeared, sitting in a massive, crumbling stone throne. The figure was dark as night. His black, thin fingers rubbed the cracked and broken arms of the old chair.

"Phan-non. No. Fellon," she whispered to herself. "My Legions and I are coming for you. We will take back Gaeya!"

The Grand One turned with a jerk and walked toward the exit. The small red pouch carrying the four Keys of Being, swaying to and fro from her waist.

CHAPTER 9

NICKY'S NEW ROLE

Awaiting the Grand One's return, new soldier Nicky, paced outside the palace. It was so strange to be in this enlarged frame, covered completely in gold armor. *Wow, wings! How was he to use them*? Just the weight on his shoulders seemed so tremendously odd. He felt somewhat off-balance. Facing the evil head-on to rescue Brin-dah and Der-rex was like deja vu. Only when he had tried to rescue Molly and his dog, he was young and very naive. The danger was only secondary then, but now he was older and able to see the menacing risk he would be taking. *What kind of powers do I possess*? He hoped Brem-mer will be able to instruct him. These sudden thoughts made him excited at first, but the realization of facing many evil sorcerers in their fortress caused him to shake with foreboding fear.

Brem-mer, knowing what lie ahead, stood at attention. He spent his entire existence protecting life, even losing his mate to an evil sorcerer. That was a Fae-ren's purpose. He had lived thousands of years. He understood this fight must be won or all life could be extinguished. This will be the most difficult, demanding role a Fae-ren could ever play: helpful, peaceful spirit now turned into a--fighting soldier. He shuddered at the thought but understood how important it was that they win.

Glymirra, still disturbed by the visions in the magical crystal, approached Nicky and Bremm-mer with the location of Fellon's Lair. "I have sent a message to the North Wind to assist you in your travel there. But once you arrive, you two will be on your own until I come with reinforcements. Use your powers and your wit to enter there. Try to hide when necessary. Nicky, you now can become invisible. Brem-mer knows this. So just close your eyes and will yourself. Much of your powers will come from your mind. Remember you are now stronger than a normal mortal. Do not panic. The fortress has many sorcerers and many enchanted animals. Try to avoid them when possible. Secrecy will bide you more time. But if you cannot stay hidden, use your sword only when necessary. Just point it at the animal or sorcerer and think "bind." They will automatically freeze and become tied-up.

"I will come with my legions as soon as Gaeya begins to heal, and the North Wind's twin is restored to his proper position. I will give you an orb so you can leave Wren and ride with the wind." With a circular motion of the index finger of her right hand an orb appeared around Nicky's neck.

Glymirra closed her eyes as she summoned the wind. "Touch your orbs now."

The Grand One waved her hand and Nicky and Brem-mer began their journey, riding on the wind. It was a very strange feeling for Nicky, who was nervously trying to cope with maintaining his equilibrium. The wind was like a wild, untamed creature that he was trying to hold onto. Brem-mer showed him how to grab on to the spirit force moving them, to act like he was riding a horse. This provided him with more support. He smiled at Brem-mer for the help and tried to go with the flow.

It was only a few minutes before they arrived. The wind set them down behind a rock formation not far from the old, mountain fortress. Snow was falling all around them. The two must now form a plan to enter the structure without being seen or felt.

"Brem-mer, I want to see if I can will myself to disappear and be more like a Fae-ren. Also, I want to try to fly with these wings before we travel closer to the Fortress. If I can practice a few times I may feel more confident. All this magical stuff is very new and overwhelming. Remember, I am just an ordinary teenage human. Nothing special about me."

Brem-mer shook his head in a negative motion. "You know Nicky there is nothing ordinary about you. That is why the Grand One and the Key chose you. I will assist you with your practice. It is wise of you to recognize you need help using your new powers."

Supernatural spirit creatures like Brem-mer could adjust to any magical change without practice. It came naturally to them, so in his new role as a golden soldier, he was comfortable.

Brem-mer watched as Nicky willed himself invisible. The first time he just flickered. The second time only part of him vanished, but it wasn't until the fourth try that he had totally disappeared. "Very good." said the Fae-ren. "Now try to fly."

The teen really had to concentrate to flap his wings. As he flapped his wings he began to move up and down in an awkward fashion, then stumbled three or four times on landings. It was several more times until he felt comfortable enough to use his wings. He really wanted to practice longer, but he knew they were already running out of time to save Der-rex and Brin-dah.

Brem-mer prompted Nicky forward. "We must now proceed closer to the Fortress with the outmost caution. We are extremely outnumbered. Let us survey the perimeter outside the main gate and find a safe spot to watch who is going in and out. Maybe we can slip inside without being noticed and locate an unguarded door or window. It is good the windows of this fortress are so large. You should not have any problem flying into one if we need to."

The two moved slowly toward the side of the ancient building's crumbling stone wall. There they found a large pile of rocks, which they hid behind as they surveyed the comings and goings of the fortress. It would give these new soldiers an idea of what they would be facing when they entered.

As they watched the entrance, a streak of red flame flew past them. It stopped in front of a very large wooden door, which led inside the Fortress. Nicky and Brem-mer looked at each other in surprise. *What was that?!*

CHAPTER 10

THE NORTH WIND'S TWIN

The Grand One took a deep breath, hoping that all would soon be peaceful now that her spirit creatures could hold their own against the rising evil. "The battles must be won! The destruction and loss of life must be stopped. I will begin my journey to The Altar of Hope as soon as I know the North Wind has been rescued and returned to his twin. I will leave without an escort. It will be quicker."

In the meantime, one hundred golden Fae-ren soldiers landed on the small island off the coast of Antarctica. It only took a brief moment for them to be spotted by the few powerful sorcerers, who were holding the North Wind prisoner with their intense combined spell.

Without warning, a freezing gale appeared out of nowhere, surrounding them. Sleet showered down on them in thick waves, until they became engulfed in ice, looking like frozen statues. The lead Protector soldier sent a telepathic message to all the frozen Fae-rens to join powers in an effort to quickly free themselves. Trusting that their new powers would release the spell, they all began chanting together. In less than five seconds they all burst free, large shards of ice flying everywhere.

The evil sorcerers turned around as they heard the ice explode and were shocked by what they saw. What were these glowing armor-clad spirits with amazing power? They vaguely resembled Fae-rens, but their auras were a bright, shining gold. Suddenly one of the sorcerers became flaming red and disappeared.

The others fought the Fae-rens, using thunderbolts which flew at great speed. Some sinister ones spoke dark incantations to thwart them. But the golden shields held by the spirits protected them, as the bolts bounced off.

The Fae-rens lined up with their shields held in front of them, creating a wall. They began to slowly march closer and closer to the ice cave, which held the captured North Wind. The sorcerers kept on blasting the golden soldiers with spells and deadly lightning and thunderbolts, but they could not keep them from advancing. Two sorcerers were even hit by their own bolts as they deflected off the Fae-rens' shields, and the Dark Ones immediately collapsed. Seeing this, panic soon overtook the remaining Evil Ones, and they began to scatter. Many turned flaming red and disappeared, trying to save themselves and in turn, left their prisoner unguarded.

In a short time, the golden soldiers of Wren reached the huge ice cave, housing the North Wind. As they approached the entrance, they heard a low humming noise coming from inside. Upon entering, they found the great wind under a strong spell, in a catatonic state in order to keep it under control. Now they must again join powers to break the strong spell.

The one hundred soldiers made a circle around the gigantic force. Ordered by the lead Fae-ren, they all began to flap their golden wings and focused their minds, thinking "dissa, dissa, dissa" which means *release*. Their combined strong supernatural powers soon broke the spell, and the North Wind slowly awakened from his magical-induced sleep.

The great being looked around and was startled by the appearance of the Golden Soldiers of Wren. It took the North Wind several minutes to remember that fifty evil sorcerers had attacked him and held him prisoner under their strong spells. Unfortunately, he didn't remember freezing Gaeya's tropical lands.

One of the Fae-ren soldiers stepped forward to explain that

the Earth was in an ice age in the south and needed to warm up fast. Could the North Wind help? They would guard him on his return to the North Pole to unite him with his Twin.

The North Wind agreed to help. So, the Fae-rens all hitched a ride on the Wind as he began the swift journey north. As they reached the tropics, the great North Wind blew a swirl of wind like a tornado, around and around the freezing lands, removing the ice and cold as it rotated. The Fae-rens were glad to see greenery appear all around them. They continued north and quickly united the North Wind with his twin. The Fae-rens then touched their orbs to head home to Wren to await further orders.

The lead Fae-ren soldier sent a telepathic message to Glymirra to let her know they had achieved success, and the North Winds' twin was safely back at the North Pole. The soldier also told the Grand One of the sorcerer that turned flaming red and disappeared soon after their arrival on the icy island. He may have alerted Fellon of their presence.

CHAPTER 11

THE ALTAR OF HOPE

Glymirra was pleased with news regarding the North Wind twin's return, but she knew Fellon would be furious at his escape. Now she must hurry to the Grotto and place the four Keys of Being in the triangular Altar of Hope. This would finally set Gaeya's balance, weaken all the evil sorcerers' powers and also release the animals under their enchantments.

In an instant Glymirra changed into an invisible form and flew out of Wren carrying the four Keys with her. With the added benefit of stronger magic from the Powerous spell, everything she did was amplified. In fact, in less than a mortal minute and with the utmost silence, Glymirra arrived above the Grotto that she had sealed many years before.

Using her magic, the great ruler waved her right hand. The earth opened up, and the entrance of the Grotto appeared before her. She quickly entered and sealed the solid earthen doorway behind her. It was crucial that no one, friend or foe, enter while she placed the Keys into the Altar. The secrets here must never be revealed.

As she began her descent through the Grotto toward the Altar of Hope, she received a telepathic message that the war raging between the Legions and Sorcerers was intensifying. Even with armor and stronger magic she was still losing Fae-rens and felt a sharp pain as each aura was snuffed out. The need to restore the keys was urgent.

She began flying at a super speed, in a downward, spiral motion, moving several thousand meters toward the center of Gaeya. It was mere blips, seconds to a mortal, when she reached the triangular Altar in the inner Earth. It was a perfect triangle, measuring four feet on each side. It was made of a solid, milky crystal that rested on a large slab of granite. Within the perfect triangle was a smaller one in the center. It contained three triangular holes to insert each key, which formed a fourth, inner triangle for the last key. Each key must be placed in a special order to achieve the proper balance.

The Ruler of Wren reached into the red sack that she carried and pulled out the four keys, shaped like long, three-dimensional triangles. The Grand One took the Pera, the pearl key of the Seas, and placed it in the topmost point of the triangle. Next, she took the Torka, a turquoise stone representing the five winds, and set it in the west point of the triangle. She repeated this process with the Gara, the red key of fire, and slid it in the east point of the small inner triangle of the Altar. Finally, the last and binding key, the amber Elka, the key of healing and rebirth, was set in the center of the triangle that was formed by the other keys. As the Elka was placed in its designated slot, a loud boom sounded, and the air around the Keys began to crackle with static electricity, creating a golden outline around the Keys as they sat in the Altar.

Glymirra knew it was time. She took a deep breath, and concentrating with all her being, she spoke the words that would awaken the power of the Keys, as she waved her hand over them and a blazing wind swirled around and around the crystal Altar. The ground shook violently. The warm wind howled eerily in the silent Grotto. Suddenly, a brilliant light appeared inside the wind tornado, lighting up the entire Grotto. In an instant, it became a flaming beast, with the head and body of a dragon and a gushing stream of water for a tail. Giant eagles' wings erupted on its back. The wings began to flap up and down, faster and faster, until the creature bounded out of the Grotto toward the surface of Gaeya at phenomenal speed, faster than the speed of light.

Magically the earth opened, and the element creature screamed, exhaling fire as it exited the deep cavern and flew into the sky, leaving behind an ear-piercing echo. All of Gaeya shook as it climbed higher and higher above the planet beginning its journey of healing. The strange supernatural creature traveled faster than any object known to mortals, as it circled the circumference of the Earth, setting the balance once again. Its tail doused fires. Its flaming breath sealed huge cracks in the earth, and its mammoth wings calmed the seas and cleared the ash-filled clouds from the sky, caused by the many volcanic eruptions.

Not wanting to waste time, Glymirra also left the Grotto, her hand sealing the entrance once more. She had won this part of the war, but there was still much work to do. As the creature healed Gaeya, the power of the evil forces would begin to weaken, and her Golden Legions would soon be much stronger than the sorcerers.

The Grand One had completed her first task. Now, she was ready to join Nicky and Brem-mer at Fellon's lair to liberate Der-rex and Brin-dah before he could destroy them. She gathered up all her commanding powers, then spread her huge wings, and took to the sky, searching for the fortress of the dark sorcerer, Fellon.

As she traveled the majestic ruler glided over mountain tops and what was left of the many forests. Glymirra surveyed the destruction of all the lands, caused by fires from volcanic eruptions and massive earthquakes. She noted the damage to the seas by incredible tsunamis. All the disasters were increased by the imbalance and some were even created by the Evil One himself.

Trees were burned or mowed down in the woodlands; fish and sea animals were washed up on shore, dead or dying. Thousands of dead birds could be seen scattered everywhere. Human structures all over the world lay in crumpled ruins. Large cracks had opened in the Earth, running down miles of coast lines and mountains.

A few thousand mortals had lost their lives by this time and several thousand more were injured, while many others were still in hiding from the environmental disasters, not knowing that rising evil forces, combined with the planet's imbalance had caused many of these anomalies. As Glymirra soared high above treetops she was saddened by all the carnage and wreckage on Gaeya that she saw. But the Grand One knew all would soon be healed by the element creature from the Altar of Hope. His incredible powers of healing and rebirth would set it all right.

Still flying high above the treetops as she continued her quest, she began to see and feel the invisible healing of the Keys' colossal supernatural beast. Fires were extinguished on all the continents; the earthquakes had stopped; the seas were beginning to calm, with the high tides slowly ebbing; and the strong winds were now becoming just gentle breezes. She smiled and continued on.

CHAPTER 12

THE PLUMP SORCERER

While Glymirra was surveying the return of the balance to Earth, the flame that stopped at the large wooden door of Fellon's Fortress, turned into a plump, dark-hooded sorcerer. As Nicky and Bremmer watched they saw the Dark One banging on the door with his fists, trying to gain entry. Trying to throw fire balls at the door and waving his hand, it appeared as if his magic could not open this door.

"It must be protected by some special magic." Brem-mer told Nicky, as the two looked at each other, wondering what was going on.

Nicky was confused. "How can we get in, if it is protected by magic?"

"Remember we have strong magic, too. If we work together, anything is possible. He must be a lesser sorcerer. The Cursed One may not give all his sorcerers automatic entrance to his lair. Only his most trusted and more powerful ones may have immediate access. Something must have happened. Let us watch and see if more sorcerers appear."

The sorcerer, still at the door, began to shout, "I must see the Cursed One now. Some strange glowing, winged spirit soldiers are trying to rescue the North Wind. Their magic is very strong. I don't think we can stop them. They were mowing us down in our tracks!"

The large door creaked open, and he scurried in. Several sorcerers moved out of the way and let him through to the stairs. He became a flame of red again, disappearing and reappearing at the door of Fellon. The chubby sorcerer, almost afraid to tell the Cursed One about the spirit soldiers, hesitated for a moment, then knocked. A deep voice said, "Enter."

The Dark One slowly opened the door with his magical finger. As he began to walk toward the Cursed One, Fellon stood up. He wheeled around to see who had entered, his empty eyes piercing. The deep raspy voice spoke, "You better have good news, Braker."

Bowing very low, the short, fat sorcerer gulped loudly and replied, "Your Darkness, I...I...do not. Glymirra is trying to free the North Wind. She sent some kind of...spirit soldiers.

They have great fighting powers. My Evil Ones seem unable to stop them. I do not know if they can keep these super soldiers away from the icy cave where we have the Wind imprisoned. We need your help."

Fellon, yelled in fury. "Why are you here?! You need to return now! Take some more Dark Ones and secure the North Wind immediately. Do not fail me on this." His booming voice caused everything around them to shake, and the lesser sorcerer cowered. Trembling with fear and afraid to look up, the chubby sorcerer stepped back, bowed quickly, then turned flaming red and disappeared.

Enraged, Fellon sat back down and began pointing his index finger at small stone statues on a ledge above him. Anger swelled up inside him. With every point of his finger a statue exploded, as if they were targets that he was shooting.

"It's a trick. Glymirra is trying to scare me. There are no such super Fae-rens. I must find an opening into Wren soon!"

In a demanding voice, he summoned Shredd. "I need you, now!"

In two seconds, Shredd appeared in front of Fellon, shaking and bowing so low he almost touched the floor. "Yes, Cursed

One. How may I be of service?"

"Find that entrance into Wren or feel my wrath. Take as many Dark Ones as you need to the cooper mine and search every inch until you find that portal! That boy was there for a reason."

In an instant Shredd flamed-up red and was gone.

As soon as Shredd disappeared, several more dark-cloaked beings appeared outside the Cursed One's open door, none brave enough to enter.

Finally, one of them spoke, his voice trembling, "Evil One, the North Wind's twin has been taken from us. We fought these strange golden spirit creatures, but we could not stop them. They were too powerful. We lost two of our brethren, when they shot lightning bolts at the creatures. Their powers and magical shields are immense."

Fellon, unable to control his ire, whirled around on them pointing his finger. His anger so great that he struck down five of them in a flash. The rest of the sorcerers immediately scattered and flamed out of the tower.

"Glymirra! This is her doing. I will find the entrance to Wren now!" He growled.

CHAPTER 13

SORCERERS ASSEMBLED

Fellon the Cursed, still enraged that the North Wind had been rescued, knew he had to find a way into Wren soon. Using his wicked powers, he summoned the gold disk which rested on a nearby shelf. He first tried to pry open the solid gold opulan using his powerful strength. Then he cursed it with many evil spells, which just pinged off its smooth surface. Finally, he used his magic to crush it open, pulling a very large brick off the stone wall and watching it slam on top of the opulan, with a loud bang echoing through the room.

Summoning the disk into his hand, the Dark One carefully examined it. Not a scratch was on it, and it remained sealed shut. He became infuriated. None of his impressive magic could touch it. How could Glymirra's powers be stronger than his? In a rage he threw the gold disk violently against one of the stone walls. It bounced off, remaining solid and intact. He was not aware that the opulans were originally given to Glymirra from the supernatural world. They were created to resist any damage and any evil spell, no matter how strong. As the Evil One sat fuming in his crumbling throne, he suddenly felt that something was very wrong. He felt a quick twinge in his chest, and his power seemed to waver quickly and then return to normal. He thought it was odd, but then went back to trying to determine how to breach Wren without the opulan to open the portal.

Again, he felt a flicker of power loss. Now, he was getting annoyed. *What was happening?* Just then, he heard a noise and looked up to see several sorcerers standing in the doorway, nervously shuffling their feet and looking at the floor.

One brave Dark One spoke up. "Cursed One, we are feeling strangely weak, and the animals are not obeying us. What are we to do? It is making it difficult to prepare for your assault on the Fae-rens."

Silently, Fellon stared at them from his empty eyes. Seconds later, loud, deafening crashes and angry roars could be heard throughout the lower levels of the fortress as the evil sorcerers lost total control over hundreds of animals, who were no longer held by dark spells. They began exiting any opening they could reach. Some were able to jump out of windows. Many just ran out the front door, trampling three sorcerers trying to enter, and creating a stampede down to the narrow pathway that led from the mountain fortress. As the animals continued to flee, they plowed down anything in their way.

Suddenly, it all made sense. The realization hit Fellon like a ton of bricks.

"NOOOOO! It can't be!" Fellon's loud voice could be heard echoing through the old stone fortress. Anger swelled up inside him. He had lost the North Wind's twin. He just lost his dominance over the bewitched animals. Now the Cursed One could feel all the evil powers around him weakening. Even his own sinister magic was beginning to slightly wane. Slamming his bony fist on the stone throne, he knew Glymirra had succeeded in uniting the Keys of Being, resetting the balance.

"But how did she get the fourth Key? The boy! He had the Key! He must have made it through the portal. Oh, Shredd, you fool! Glymirra will pay. I will defeat her and takeover Wren, if it's the last thing I do. I must rule over all!"

Leaving the sorcerers standing in his doorway without an explanation, he became flaming red then appeared in the Great Hall. He sat down on a large marble throne located in the middle of the room. The left arm had been broken off a few hundred years prior. He sat there mulling over a plan, talking to himself. "I must find a way to destroy Wren. Then all my Dark Ones will return to their former strength, and I will be unstoppable once more."

As he thought about what to do, the Cursed One became uncontrollably angry. Sparks began shooting out from around his hood. He cried out in a very deep, thunderous, voice which echoed throughout every room.

"My Evil Ones, join me in the Great Hall. NOW!"

As he called forth all available sorcerers, within seconds, three thousand confused Dark Ones gathered in the Great Hall, hoping that their weakening powers would be restored.

The Cursed One rose up before them, seething as he spoke, red flames now burning around his black hood. Small sparks were flying out as he raised his arms in ire.

"Glymirra has united the Keys. They are sucking our sinister strength away as they heal Gaeya. Even I feel their effects. We must find a way to stop the healing of Gaeya, before it is too late. It is the only way to get back your powers and for us to carry-on our sinister plan. My dark horde, we have lost control over the animals, but we must band together. Only by combining our dark powers, can we remain strong. I know what we must do! The boy entered a portal in the copper mine in the desert. Shredd is searching for the portal location as I speak. Taking over Wren is the only way we can defeat Glymirra and regain our hold. I will take all but five hundred dark ones with me. The rest of you will try to confuse those new soldiers all around Gaeya. You will go in groups of five and focus on the areas where animals are being helped. You will find the golden soldiers with them. Destroy as many of these warriors as you can. This will enable the rest of us to concentrate on finding the portal into Wren and taking over the magical realm."

An old hunched sorcerer, with his head hung down, shaking, almost afraid to speak, whispered "But Cursed One, I am feeling too weak." Several other sorcerers with their heads bowed, started shuffling their feet, afraid to speak. They nodded slightly in agreement.

Fellon, outraged, sparks still flying all around him, pointed his finger at the old one, destroying him and two others standing next to him. "You forget who made you strong! Now, go or face the consequences as your friend just did." They immediately turned flaming red and escaped from the hall.

He turned his hollow eyes to the rest of the Dark Ones. "Anyone else too weak to take over the world? No? Then, the rest of you will follow me to the mine in the western desert. We will meet up with Shredd. It is imperative that we find the portal to Wren where the boy entered. If you want to keep your powers and not risk my wrath, you will be there."

Just as they were about to leave, Tarr reminder the Cursed One of his two Fae-ren prisoners. "Tarr, go get them and meet us at the copper mine. They may know where the portal entrance is and how we can enter without the use of the gold disk."

Waving his arm, he turned flaming red and went to join the other sorcerers who had already gone to find Shredd.

Tarr, all alone in the ancient fortress, preceded to the dungeon to fetch the caged Fae-rens.

CHAPTER 14

THE ENCHANTED ANIMALS

As Nicky and Brem-mer began moving closer to the fortress, both suddenly halted as a mass exodus of frightened, stampeding animals began flooding the exits of the huge stone structure. Wolves, large dogs, bears of every variety, mountain lions, even white tigers came out from the great fortress, running in every direction, as they descended the mountain.

Nicky, looking perplexed, asked Brem-mer "What is going on?"

Being a magical Fae-ren, Brem-mer knew, and said, excitedly, "Oh, Guardian! The Grand One has delivered the Keys to the Altar of Hope and reset the balance! Because of this, the sorcerers are losing some of their powers. They can no longer control the animals they had bewitched. The confused and frightened animals have returned to their normal selves. We will wait for the stampede to slow, then we can approach one of the side windows of the Fortress."

Nicky and Brem-mer did not know that inside the small

dungeon cell, Brin-dah and Der-rex had found a way to escape. As soon as they opened the small wooden niche in the top of the door, Brin-dah (in her Fae-ren form) closed her eyes, placed a finger to her forehead and concentrated on Wren. She could feel a telepathic doorway was open this time, so she sent a brief message to Glymirra, asking for help. She hoped that the Grand One had received it.

Then, the two Fae-rens transformed into spiders and crawled out the tiny opening to freedom. Transforming back into Fae-ren form, the two spirit creatures slowly made their way through the hallway of the dungeon. They hugged the damp walls as they walked, fearing they might be caught by one of Fellon's sorcerers. Did Glymirra receive their message? Sending help was questionable, since the Ruler or Wren had more important things to do. They both knew they had to rely on themselves. Each time they reached an open cell door, they stopped, breathing a sigh of hope with each empty room they passed. Slowly, they moved closer and closer to the stairs going up to next level of the fortress.

CHAPTER 15

THE MINE PORTAL

Glymirra, relieved now that she had reset the balance of Gaeya, and knowing the North Wind's twin had been rescued, finally set out to the Evil One's stone fortress. She sent a message to Nicky and Brem-mer, letting them know she was on her way.

Feeling determined her blue eyes brightened as she neared the Evil One's fortress. Armed with the knowledge of who Fellon had been, she was ready to face the Dark One and rescue her Fae-rens. But as she was nearing the fortress, Kendar notified the Grand One that numerous sorcerers had gathered by the portal wall in the mine where the Guardian Nicky had entered.

Since the Centaur's magical powers had increased with the Powerous spell, he was now able feel the frigid evil lurking on the other side of the mine wall in Gaeya. The cold and wickedness were so concentrated that he was afraid Fellon may have joined them. Glymirra noted the immense fear in his message and reversed direction, on her way to Wren in a flash.

She arrived in less than thirty seconds. There was much more at stake here. She had to protect Wren. Brem-mer and Nicky were on their own. They would have to find a way to free her two most trusted Fae-rens. She summoned her Pterodactyl guard as she was landing, and he immediately arrived at the palace entrance.

"I need half of my Legions to report back to Wren, now! Summon them immediately. Fellon is trying to breach our world through the destroyed mine portal where our Guardian entered. We only have two mortal hours before our closed doorway re-aligns with the old mineshaft portal. If Fellon and his cronies unite their sinister powers, even with many in a weakened state, their evil force may be able to open it without an opulan. I sense Fellon himself still has very strong evil powers. For some reason, the magic of the Keys has not diluted his incredible strength."

As the pterodactyl hastened to summon the Golden Legions, the Grand One hurried to her quarters, located in the rear of the palace.

"I must see where Fellon is at this very moment." She approached the Reflection of Ages. Standing before it, she waved her hand and demanded, "Show me Fellon's location." The sapphire crystal clouded over then quickly cleared to show a low-ceilinged mine shaft. Dark hooded figures were moving slowly forward into the shaft, passing massive piles of rubble from a recent cave-in. Using magic to lift large timber and stone barriers, they continued through.

Distressed by the vision, Glymirra hurried out of the palace, looking for her guard. "We do not have much time. Fellon and his sorcerers are almost to the portal wall. In thirty mortal minutes our doorway aligns with the portal. At that time, with all the Evil Ones he has brought, their combined magic will be able to break through without an opulan and invade Outer Wren. We must keep them from entering Inner Wren."

About twenty thousand Protectors had just arrived in front of the palace. Glymirra immediately gave them the news and their orders. "My soldiers, you must at all costs keep the Dark Ones from entering our inner realm. I need five thousand of you to stay here and guard the Gate and the inhabitants that are hiding in Inner Wren. The rest of you will be with me in Outer Wren, awaiting the invasion of the Evil Ones. I will face Fellon alone. He is still too powerful, even for my Golden Legions. Now, go to your positions. Defend our realm. Use any and all magic you possess."

Glymirra headed out the jeweled gate, followed by several thousand of her golden soldiers. As she approached the doorway that Nicky Kirkland entered, she was greeted by Kendar and his centaurs. Kendar bowed to the Grand One.

"The icy cold is worse."

"I know. Fellon is here with several hundred sorcerers. They may be outnumbered and a little weaker since I set the balance of Gaeya, but they are strong in their beliefs. Evil doesn't need many numbers to wreak havoc on good. They will give their entire beings to become strong again. We must be cautious. Tricks and spells are their way to distract and conquer. Let your Centaurs be on their guard. I want to keep the loss of life low for both sides."

CHAPTER 16

THE DUNGEON

Outside Nicky and Brem-mer noticed the mass of fleeing animals had slowed down. Nodding to one another they started creeping closer to the fortress. Then they saw a strange sight: hundreds of red flames were streaming out of doors and windows then disappearing into the air. They knew something was going on. Would there be less sorcerers to deal with and no bewitched animals? Maybe, just maybe, they would not need Glymirra's help.

The two golden soldiers crept closer and closer, until they came upon the east wall of the fortress. There, two levels above them was a huge window. Was it protected by magic or could they just fly in? Slowly, Nicky and Brem-mer began flapping their wings. The spell used by Glymirra helped the Fae-rens to feel magical protections. It became clear as they approached that the window was not protected by any enchantments. Since this seemed odd, Brem-mer sent a look of caution to Nicky as they came closer to the opening. Nodding his head to Nicky that they would enter,

Brem-mer flew in first, followed by an anxious Nicky. The teen landed inside a long hallway, glad to be on solid ground again. *Flying should be for the birds*, he thought.

Carefully, they stopped and looked around, searching for any signs of the Dark Ones. They began to walk forward slowly, on alert for any signs of the sorcerers or Fellon himself. They passed doorway after doorway, with rooms empty, fireplaces still burning in some, straw scattered on floors and piles of bones in others, chewed by the wild animals they had enchanted.

"Strange. I don't see anyone on this floor," Nicky quietly told Brem-mer, uneasy at the silence all around.

"Don't be fooled, Nicky. Fellon is known for his element of surprise. Stay alert. We will descend to the next level. The dungeon should be below that, based on the Grand One's knowledge."

The two used great caution as they neared the crumbling stone steps to the next level, surveying their surroundings as they progressed. When they had walked the entire length of that floor, they both breathed a huge sigh of relief.

But Nicky was still uncomfortable. "Brem-mer, do you think they took Brin-dah and Der-rex wherever they were going?"

Brem-mer looked worried and responded, "I was thinking the

same thing. But just to be sure, we need to check the dungeon first. I am hoping they forgot about them. It appears they may have more important things to do since our Grand One returned the Keys. Let us continue to the next level. It should be the last level before we reach the dungeon area. Be cautious."

Meanwhile in the dungeon level, Tarr appeared. He began making his way to the last cell where he had put the cage housing the unconscious Fae-rens.

"Oh, no!" Der-rex whispered as he grabbed Brin-dah, who almost ran into Tarr. "We have to hide or make a run for the stairs." Brin-dah took his hand and telepathically told him to try for the steps to the next level. Just then Nicky and Brem-mer began making their way down the steps to the dungeon and collided with the two escaping Fae-rens.

"Whoa!" Nicky said. "It's good to see you guys. We have come to rescue you." But before anyone could move, Tarr spied them from the other end of the dungeon. Surprised and panicked by their presence, he started shooting lightning bolts and rapid spells at them, not taking time to aim. Ducking as a bolt flew past his head, the teen soldier put up his sword, pointed it at the sorcerer and thought "bind". Tarr immediately froze up, eyes wide, and an invisible golden rope bound him like a spider wrapping its prey. With a loud thud, he fell to the earthen floor.

"Wow!" Came from Brin-dah's lips. Both Fae-rens were amazed at the sight of Nicky and Brem-mer, their golden armor and strength impressive.

"Thank you for coming to our rescue. We were afraid our message was not received, since we had been here so long. We decided to try to escape on our own. We know that the Grand One is very busy, and that she is trying to restore balance to Gaeya. It is a most important task. It seems that you both have received some magical help. What is this golden armor you wear?"

Brem-mer replied "Well, the devastation was growing too fast and we were losing too many Protector Fae-rens to the Evil Ones, so the Grand One used an ancient spell to give us more powers to defeat the Dark Ones. It turned us both into these golden soldiers. In fact, all Protectors are now soldiers. We believe the Keys have been restored to the Altar in Gaeya. We also think that most of the evil sorcerers are slowly losing their sinister powers. The bewitched animals have returned to normal and this sorcerer," he pointed at Tarr, "is the only one left at this fortress. The others have left, but we're not sure where they went. We need to get out of here quickly, but first I will contact our Grand One and let her know that Nicky and I have freed you. We will all head home to Wren."

Brem-mer put his finger to his forehead to send a telepathic message to his ruler, giving her the good news. But he immediately received a terrifying response. *I am relieved to know they are well. We are in strong danger of invasion by Fellon The Cursed and many of his evil Dark Ones. They are trying to breach the portal wall where our Guardian entered. The portal and the doorway will align in a few mortal minutes. It will be quite possible for them to use their powers to open it, and we will have no choice. We can use your help. Please come as quickly as you can and be prepared to do battle!*

All four of them were shocked by this news. "We must hurry back." Brem-mer nodded to Nicky. They touched their orbs and began traveling to Wren on the winds.

CHAPTER 17

BATTLE OF WREN

The three Fae-rens and the Guardian touched down in outer Wren just as Kendar yelled, "The evil is breaking through. Everyone, raise your shields and swords. We must protect inner Wren." Ten thousand golden soldiers lined the cobblestone pathway in a battle stance, shields in front and swords drawn.

Further away, the winged centaur stationed twenty centaurs and twenty sentinels in front of the huge jeweled gate with about five thousand more warriors ready to enter and defend the gate from inside. "No one must enter that gate!" Kendar screamed.

At that moment, Nicky spotted Glymirra. She seemed larger than ever, standing seven or eight feet tall, with a golden feathered helmet and wide gold breast plate, the golden wings of Wren blazing on its front. Her talons thick and sharp, her enormous eagle wings open wide. Nicky was almost frightened at the sight of the Grand One, but he knew she was poised to fight.

Brem-mer looked at the two rescued Fae-rens. "You both need

to hide or go to the inner realm. You cannot defend yourselves against the Dark Ones without the magic of the 'Powerous.' Nicky and I will join the others in protecting our world."

Brin-dah and Der-rex knew they were no match for the sorcerers, but they would not leave. "This is our home." Brin-dah said. "We will stay and do the best we can defending it." Brem-mer slowly nodded his head, understanding their decision.

At the same time, in the copper mine Fellon stood waiting for Tarr to appear with the Fae-rens he had captured in the desert, hoping they would be able to tell him how to breach Wren without an opulan. Time was running out. With the use of his fierce powers, he touched the wall the Guardian had entered. He could feel the doorway and portal beginning to align. Without the gold disk he would have to use sheer strength and power to open the portal. The Evil One surveyed his horde, an idea forming that would allow him to breach Wren.

"Dark Ones, move yourselves to this wall now! The portal is aligning!" Many gathered next to the wall as Fellon yelled, "Lightning bolts, at the ready!" Five hundred sorcerers pointed at the wall just as the doorway of Wren became visible. "Fire!"

In unison, hundreds of hooded sorcerers released their heavily charged lightning bolts.

On the other side of the portal, Kendar felt the concentration of evil, and screamed, "Brace yourselves!" A tremendous explosion was heard. Debris from the wall flew everywhere, showering the closest Fae-rens. Then a flood of dark figures began spilling into Wren. Seriously outnumbered, the sorcerers were being halted and tied up by the large number of golden soldiers waiting for them.

Suddenly Fellon swooped in, shooting lightning bolts and yelling magical curses at as many Protectors as possible. Several soldiers were knocked down by his strong bolts, but their shields protected them from serious harm. He then disappeared into thin air, leaving his Dark Ones to continue the invasion.

Just then a new flood of sinister wizards began to flow through the portal. Their powers seemed much stronger than the first wave of Evil Ones. This made the new golden soldiers fall back from the hole in the wall. Lightning bolts fired from black, crooked fingers, flying in every direction. Some of them started fires in the fruit trees that lined the cobblestone path, other hit the cobblestone walkway like bombs going off, sending stones flying everywhere. As the Dark Ones advanced, they left many of the beautiful fields of flowers burning, and some were just mowed down.

More of the Dark Ones turned into flames and disappeared. They suddenly reappeared in surprise attacks on the Fae-ren soldiers. This made the Protectors start to fall back away from the portal entrance. Some of the Fae-ren soldiers were feeling a little apprehensive as twenty of their rank were hit at one time and fell to the ground. One was badly injured, but all the rest had perished, their auras extinguished. Until then, they had felt invincible. The sudden losses seem to slow them down, making them more hesitant as they remembered the peaceful spirits they had been until recently. They paused to look around Outer Wren and saw that their beautiful, quiet realm lay in ruin. Saddened by these images, they knew they had to protect their world.

A lead golden soldier encouraged his group to continue chasing and capturing more Dark Ones. "Remain alert! We were warned about their trickery. Remember that we are strong and powerful, too. Glymirra has given us the tools to protect Wren! Fight for your realm!" Hearing this, the others began to fight with renewed purpose. They began moving forward through clouds of smoke with swords drawn and steady, attacking more sorcerers as they moved down what was left of the cobblestone path. A few golden soldiers remained by the portal opening in case more of the evil wizards entered.

Looking on from a distance and surprised that he was losing many of his dark army, the Cursed One took shelter behind a large tree. "I need to find Glymirra," he whispered. "All will stop once I defeat her." He began scanning the area. *She must be here,* he thought.

Glymirra was looking for Fellon at the same time, knowing once he was captured the fight would end. With her increased powers, she telepathically contacted the Reflection of Ages crystal. *Show me the Cursed One.* He was hiding behind a tree about fifty yards from where she stood. Cloaking her appearance, she was able to sneak up on him.

The Grand One's massive frame began to materialize in front of Fellon. Startled, he jumped up and spouted spells and curses, left and right. Glymirra recited her own spells, and with a circle of her right finger, a sword appeared.

He looked for help from his dwindling horde. Calling them to his aid, he realized more than half of his sorcerers were captured and a some lay still on the cobblestone path. They had lost their life from rebounded spells. Seeing this and coming up with another plan, he smiled smugly at her and turned into a flame of red. He was gone in an instant, leaving Glymirra alone.

The Cursed One found Shredd who was battling two Fae-ren soldiers. Out of all his Dark Ones, Shredd still had strong dark powers. Fellon's flame whispered into Shredd's ear, "Come with me. We can ambush Glymirra and take over. All her golden soldiers will surrender to us once we have her under our control. Wren will be ours! Now gather a few of your stronger Dark Ones and join me." Shredd nodded. He became a red flame and disappeared with the Cursed One.

CHAPTER 18

FELLON'S TRICKERY

Glymirra was shocked by Fellons's retreat. *I don't trust him. He will not give-up so easily. I must be on my guard for a surprise attack. Now I need to check on my legions' progress with rounding up his Evil Ones.*

Just then the Grand One received a telepathic message stating that her soldiers on Gaeya had subdued about a hundred evil ones, while many more ran away when they saw the golden ones. Their powers were greatly weakened. The same Protector also told her how the animals had returned to their homes, the skies were clearing and returning to their normal blue color, and the oceans were calming. She smiled at the great news and knew they had won the battle on Gaeya.

Five yards from the portal entrance, Nicky and Brem-mer had stopped many sorcerers trying to enter or leave. The pair of golden soldiers had become regular fighting machines. Their new swords provided them with much success, allowing them to easily stop the robed figures in their tracks and bind them up like a neat package. Most of these Dark Ones' powers had weakened a great deal. The sorcerers moved slowly giving them little time to fight back.

The pair looked around for more sorcerers to capture. As Nicky scanned the area, he became shaken at the sight, noticing that the beautiful, peaceful Wren he had entered two days ago, was destroyed. Huge trees were down, some burning; the endless fields of flowers were almost gone, too. Smoke was billowing up in the sky. The cobblestone pathway was left in pieces. Debris lay everywhere. He shook his head in disbelief and sadness. But the fight was not over.

Just then, the young Guardian caught sight of Brin-dah and Der-rex trying to fight off two Dark Ones. They were having a difficult time, with only their normal Fae-ren magic. Brin-dah ducked, nearly hit by a bolt of lightning. Nicky stopped Brem-mer and pointed to the struggling Fae-rens. Brem-mer nodded, and the two soldiers hurried to rescue them. They pointed their swords at the Evil Ones and subdued them quickly.

Brin-dah, tired and relieved, smiled at her two saviors. But Brem-mer reminded them that this battlefield was no place for

Protectors that were not soldiers. Nicky agreed. "You should move to the inner realm where you will be protected. Please go. We don't want to worry about you, too."

Der-rex and Brin-dah looked at one another, then agreed to take shelter away from the fight. Waving goodbye to Brin-dah and Der-rex, they continued fighting and capturing more sorcerers, moving further into Wren toward the jeweled gate. While binding yet another Dark One, Nicky felt a chill go down his spine. Something was wrong. He looked at Brem-mer. "Have you seen Glymirra recently?"

Brem-mer looked thoughtfully at him. "No," The Fae-ren responded.

"I hope she is alright."

"Don't worry, Guardian. Our ruler is very powerful. She can take care of herself. In fact, she may be looking for Fellon."

"Yeah, I haven't seen him either. Shredd disappeared, too. Do you think it is a trick?"

Brem-mer frowned. "I hope not. I think we should move closer to the gate which opens into Inner Wren. Maybe we will find our ruler there. I have noticed the fighting in front of the jeweled gate has increased. It seems that many sorcerers have suddenly appeared there. At least we can help the Centaurs and the Sentinel hawks, whom now seem to be struggling on this side of the gate."

Many golden soldiers waited on the inner side of the gate, poised to stop any sorcerer who might make it through. The animal inhabitants of Wren were still hidden safely far away from all the fighting, along with the worker Fae-rens. All were anxiously awaiting the outcome of this war.

Feeling determined, Nicky looked at Brem-mer and said, "Ok, let's do this." The pair spread their golden wings and flew to the jeweled gate. The two of them jumped right into the conflict, shields deflecting spells and binding up Dark Ones. A few of the sorcerers still displayed tremendous powers, and they had to work together to subdue each one.

Kendar nodded in thanks. He was fighting two sorcerers at a time, but he was also tiring. He was the one who sent the golden soldiers inside the gate, when the fighting increased, knowing they needed to protect Inner Wren at all costs.

Suddenly Fellon appeared at the ornate gate to Inner Wren. Then Shredd and about thirty more sorcerers appeared out of nowhere, standing in front of him. They were shooting thunderbolts and sending curses at the Centaurs, who now seemed very overwhelmed. In fact, several of their comrades were hit and now lay on the ground.

Without warning, Glymirra showed up spouting ancient incantations and using her mighty sword, effortlessly overtaking several sorcerers. Nicky yelled to Brem-mer, then pointing to the Grand One who had entered the fight. She sent a telepathic message to all the Wren fighters at the gate. *Keep them out of Inner Wren, if you can. Fellon is mine!*

But Fellon laughed with a wicked sound, echoing throughout Wren. He had Glymirra right where he wanted her. He nodded to Shredd, thinking, *we have her now.* He moved in very close to the Grand One. As soon as she turned to him, he disappeared, taking some of the Dark Ones with him. She stood still for a moment to assess what she saw, her large blue eyes widening, as she realized, *he must be playing cat and mouse with me. I must be on guard for his trickery.*

As the Centaurs and Sentinels continued to fight all around, Nicky paused for a minute. He knew something wasn't right. Everyone around him was still fighting, but there were suddenly less Evil Ones. They just disappeared again. Where did they go? "Oh, No. I don't like this."

He hurried over to Brem-mer to alert him of the changed situation. Brem-mer stopped immediately, nervously looking for Glymirra. There she was, leaning up against the left side of the Gate, watching and waiting for Fellon to reappear. In the meantime, using her powers, Glymirra reached out to the Reflection of Ages and was able to see her foe, cloaked and approaching her.

"It's a trap!" Brem-mer screamed. Nicky realized the Fae-ren was right and moved swiftly toward the Grand One. But it was too late! She was surrounded by Fellon, Shredd, and about thirty other sorcerers. Fellon, laughed loudly. "We have you now!"

The two golden soldiers halted five yards from them. What were they to do? Nicky was in shock, "She cannot handle all of them herself."

"I think the Evil One planned it that way," Brem-mer retorted. "We may need Kendar's help. Maybe he can open the jeweled gate so we can get reinforcements on this side again. I know it is risky, since we don't want anyone in Inner Wren, but this is our leader we're talking about! I will contact him telepathically and explain the terrifying circumstance."

Brem-mer closed his eyes, put his finger to his forehead and reached out for Kendar. *Our leader is in trouble. Can you send anyone to help?* Kendar agreed to quickly assess the situation.

But the Grand One expected the ambush. She stood stoic, her blue eyes staring fiercely. Without warning, a loud piercing sound came from her mouth. Alarmed, Fellon yelled to his Dark Ones, "Don't let her move her arms. Keep her from using magic against us. Move in!"

All of a sudden, a violent windstorm blew in around them. Even Nicky and Brem-mer felt the rough wind from where they stood. It distracted the sorcerers for only a second. But in that second Glymirra flapped her mammoth eagle wings and created an explosive discharge. It was like a huge bomb had just detonated. All the Evil Ones around her flew high into the air, then fell to the ground with a thud, several yards away. None of them were moving. But as she looked around, Fellon and Shredd had somehow escaped again.

Yards away, Nicky stood, his eyes wide and his mouth open in awe of the Grand Ones' power. Brem-mer saw the adoration in the teen's eyes and commented with pride, "I told you our ruler is very, very powerful."

Just as the two soldiers started to move toward Glymirra, she disappeared.

"Where is she going?" Nicky asked Brem-mer.

"I don't know, but we need to keep moving."

A few seconds later Kendar approached them. "We could use your help in the inner realm. I just received a message that two sorcerers have been spotted close to the palace. I only opened the gate for a second when I received your message. Then I saw that our Grand One had already defeated the Evil Ones. We also are getting flooded again with more of them on this side of the gate."

Looking around, they noticed more sorcerers, shooting thunderbolts at the Centaurs and Sentinels they encountered, with the more powerful ones firing lightning bolts. Some were so close they hit the gate, and red, white and blue crystals flew off. Luckily, the strong, magical frame of the golden gate would be difficult to damage.

"I will need some of the golden soldiers I assigned to Inner Wren to help us. I lost several of my Sentinels and a few of my Centaurs in the last wave."

As the fighting continued around them, the teen saw several

massive hawks lying on the ground a few feet from where he stood. Some injured, some dead. He was having a hard time dealing with all these losses. He was just a teenager, after all. All this death and destruction was very distressing to him. Brem-mer hid the fact that he too was deeply saddened. He did not want this fifteen-year-old soldier to quit on him. He knew it was a lot for a young mortal to handle. But he also knew the Guardian was strong. Brem-mer motioned to the teen to come closer to the jeweled gate. They were ready to help.

Kendar told Nicky and Brem-mer he would open the gate for two mortal seconds to let the golden soldiers exit, who would help outside the gate. "You must enter Inner Wren at the same time. I cannot open this gate again until everyone is safe, and the fighting is done."

Kendar signaled to another Centaur to open the gate just far enough to let two hundred golden soldiers into the outer realm, while Nicky and Brem-mer stepped inside the inner sanctum of Wren.

CHAPTER 19

THE PALACE SANCTUARY

Nicky was amazed that it was calmer and quieter here. The battle had not touched Inner Wren. The trees, bushes and lush grasslands were intact. Marble benches and pathways were pristine. The sky was blue, not black from smoke. He took a deep breath and to his surprise, it smelled like freshly mowed grass and flowers. Not at all like the smell of death and smoke on the other side. No one was fighting. He could see the several hundred remaining golden soldiers stationed at the gate. But the rest of the inner realm was uninhabited. No animals or worker Fae-rens were visible. It was empty of life as far as the eye could see. Everyone was in hiding.

The Guardian and Brem-mer began moving toward the palace to hunt for the sorcerers that Kendar had mentioned. They had last been seen in this area. The two golden soldiers continued forward, stopping every few seconds to scan ahead of them. So far, they had found nothing out of the ordinary.

But Fellon was smart. If he couldn't capture Glymirra on the other side, he knew the gate might open to protect her. As soon as the jeweled gate opened a crack, he was ready and pulled Shredd in with him. They were cloaked so they would not be seen, as they moved behind a large pillar to hide away from the Fae-ren soldiers. He quietly explained his plan to Shredd. The Cursed One would draw out the Ruler of Wren, and Shredd would be ready to strike. Then, Wren would be his!

The two sorcerers turned into red flames and sped toward the palace. Once there, they cloaked themselves to avoid being seen and waited at the entrance for the Grand One to show up. However, as they were hiding, invisible to everyone, Brem-mer and Nicky made it to front of the palace sanctuary.

Brem-mer whispered to the teen, "We will search the right side of the sanctuary together. If we do not find anyone, we will split-up." Nicky nodded in agreement. He followed Brem-mer, who was more experienced with the layout of the palace. The two of them slowly and cautiously checked around the entire front of the large marble palace, as they made their way along the wall of the right side. Brem-mer suddenly put out his arm, to stop Nicky for a moment. He thought he felt a frigid spot as he approached the right side of the palace--a sure sign of evil. Slowly and quietly he drew his sword, waiting for any movement. Nothing happened, and the cold dissipated. The two soldiers relaxed and continued walking.

But the shrewd Cursed One, still cloaked, nodded to Shredd and moved swiftly to the outer end of the palace, unnoticed.

"What was that all about?" Nicky asked Brem-mer.

"The Evil Ones were here but have moved from this area. I felt the cold they left behind. They must be using a cloaking spell to remain invisible. Be on your guard for attack. They could be anywhere. I fear it is Fellon or some of his more power sorcerers. I think we need to remain together. It would be dangerous at this time to split-up."

"That's fine with me." Nicky responded feeling a little nervous. He wasn't too keen on facing Fellon, even with his new powers. This guy was the stuff of nightmares. Nicky shuddered, remembering the cursed animals he had sent after Nicky when he was only ten years old. *But where is Glymirra?* he thought.

At the same time, the Grand One was in her chambers at the back of the palace, using the Reflection of Ages to check on all the fighting in Outer Wren. Her Golden Legions were winning, but she had lost more soldiers, centaurs and hawks. Setting the balance of Gaeya did not weaken as many sorcerers as she had hoped. The only way to stop the evil takeover now was for her to use the powers given to her when Gaeya was created. Now it was time to take Fellon head on, using herself as bait. The Grand One needed to get him out in the open. But where? The blue crystal showed her that he was hiding by the left side of the palace behind a large column. He was by himself. *There must be a few other sorcerers hiding close by,* she thought. *He never goes alone.*

Now ready to face her foe, the Ruler of Wren, still dressed in her impressive battle gear, walked confidently to the palace entrance with her sword drawn. Just as she stepped out the entrance, Shredd, who was hiding nearby behind a fruit tree, shot a powerful thunderbolt at her. Using her supernatural powers was she able to deflect it away from her with a flick of her hand. It hit a marble bench that exploded on contact. She looked around quickly, searching for Fellon. But he remained hidden, waiting for the right moment to strike.

Tired of his games, Glymirra called him out. "Fellon, come out and face me now! Just you and me. We have both lost many of our comrades. We need to finish this now."

She waited a few moments, but there was no response. Trying another attack, Glymirra goaded him. "Is the great, powerful Cursed One afraid of the Ruler of Wren?"

She had struck a nerve. "No one calls me a coward and lives!" a loud, deep voice roared! Fellon sent a very forceful, thunderous, lightning bolt at the Grand One, almost knocking her down. She wavered for a second. It was just enough time for Fellon to suddenly emerge in front of her, cursing her with strong magic. A second later, Shredd appeared on top of her, attempting to tie-up her massive wings. One of the dark spells spoken by the Cursed One made it impossible for Glymirra to speak. The ruler realized she had underestimated their strength and began to struggle. As she attempted to raise her sword, Fellon sent another bolt from his fingers, knocking it into the air. It landed a few feet from her.

In the meantime, Nicky and Brem-mer heard all the booms from the thunderbolts. Immediately they stopped their search and ran to the other side of the palace, not knowing what they would find. They were shocked at what they saw. Wren's great ruler was in danger!

But with everything going on, no one noticed the pair. Brem-mer silently pointed to Nicky to sneak up on Fellon and Shredd. Nicky nodded and they slowly crept towards the battle in front of them.

"You're weak! I am the powerful one! We have you now. This world is mine!" Fellon screamed in sinister voice. "My Evil Ones will be strong and rule both worlds. Every creature will bow to me!"

Glymirra's eyes widened with anger as she continued to struggle. Shredd had her completely tied-up. Without her hands, wings or her voice, she would have a difficult time getting out of this situation by herself. Unfortunately for the Cursed One, Brem-mer and Nicky silently moved behind the two Evil Ones, suddenly pointing their swords at the same time. One at Fellon and one at Shredd. The swords immediately froze them in place. Then the golden soldiers quickly bound them up like a spider when it catches its prey. They dropped to the ground, eyes wide and furious, in shock at being captured.

Nicky ran over to Glymirra and untied her, while Brem-mer stood guard over the two Sorcerers, his sword pointed at them. No one could trust the Cursed One. But hopefully his tricks had ended. Brem-mer telepathically told Kendar that they had captured the dark leader and his most powerful sidekick. With her hands free, Glymirra reversed the curse on her voice and sent a message to the entire world of Wren, that Fellon had been captured. Her very loud voice echoed the victory!

Everyone, Golden Soldiers and Dark Ones alike stopped fighting. After hearing the Cursed One had been captured, the sorcerers began to surrender. The Golden Legions of Wren raised their swords and cheered. The war was finally over!

But there was still much to do.

Kendar and his Centaurs opened the jeweled gate. Soldiers began to pour into Inner Wren. He dispatched several of them to retrieve all the fallen and the injured and bring them into the inner realm. Their ruler would heal all the wounded with her magic, and all the fallen would be laid to rest in one of the endless fields of flowers.

Hearing that the battle was over, the worker Fae-rens and some of the animal inhabitants slowly began to come out of hiding. Fae-ren soldiers and workers started to gather by the palace sanctuary. Brin-dah and Der-rex also came out of hiding. Everyone stopped to see the captured Cursed One but kept their distance. Nicky and Brem-mer stayed close to Glymirra, guarding the two captured sorcerers.

Now it was time to decide Fellon's fate. Many Fae-rens stood close by, waiting to hear justice delivered by their great leader. The Grand One's large frame stood in front of the Evil One. Her big eyes stared in sadness as they looked into his soul. Then she addressed him." The Reflection of Ages crystal revealed to me, that you were once Phan-non, leader to my Fae-rens, a great Protector and my special aid."

Surprise and shock shown on every face there.

"Though it appears you are the darkest of all sorcerers, I know it was not your choice to become evil. You were cursed repeatedly until your aura died and great evil was forced into your being. I have weighed the atrocities you have done in the last seventy-five mortal years. They are inexcusable, but I will show you mercy.

"I have consulted the 'Powerous: Book of Extreme Incantations.' It will be a great process, but it has the power to reverse the curse done unto you. Unfortunately, I cannot return any Fae-ren powers to you. You will be spared and turned into a worker Fae-ren."

Then she turned to Shredd. "I will release you and the other sorcerers, but I will drain your powers before you go. It will be many, many long years before you will regain them, and you will never be as powerful as you once were."

Kendar and some of his centaurs were by the palace, listening to their ruler speak. The Grand One turned to Kendar, "Please have some of the centaurs and my soldiers escort all the captured sorcerers to the front of the palace. They can be released once I have taken their powers from them. Make sure they are escorted out of Wren and that the portal wall is resealed on both sides. I don't want anyone to be able to find it again."

Glymirra walked into the palace. Everyone waited for her return. In the meantime, all the captured sorcerers were led into the inner realm and marched up to the front of the palace to receive their sentences. The Golden Legions delivered several hundred captured Evil Ones to the Palace Sanctuary. There the remaining Protector Fae-rens lined-up in squad formation.

Everyone wanted to witness the disarming of the sorcerers' evil strength. All the worker Fae-rens and most of the animal inhabitants stood several yards away, watching and waiting. Nicky stood near Brem-mer, still guarding Fellon and Shredd.

He began to look around. He was amazed to see Inner Wren this crowded. Extremely tired but relieved, he looked at Brem-mer and smiled.

A few minutes later Glymirra walked out of the palace entrance. She no longer wore armor. Now she had her royal cape over her shoulders and the large, golden "Powerous" in her hand. She waved her hand and a lectern appeared. She was finally ready, as she opened the book and set it down.

CHAPTER 20

THE TRANSFORMATION

The Grand One raised her hands to bring silence and order to the crowd before her. "I know it has been a very difficult and trying time for all of you. We will now bring it to end. I will perform two very special incantations to help reverse the evil that has plagued us for many years. One will drain the powers from the captured sorcerers. The other very difficult spell will transform Fellon, formerly our Phan-non, to a harmless worker Fae-ren. He will never do evil deeds again." Loud cheers were heard coming from everywhere in Wren.

Glymirra again raised her large hand, and everyone calmed down.

Standing very still, all listened as the Ruler of Wren began speaking the strange ancient language on the gold page. It was not in words but somber musical melodies. The wind blew, circling the large group of bound up sorcerers, who were trembling at the thought of losing their powers. Tiny white lights materialized from above. They descended like falling stars until they stopped on top of each Evil Ones' head. Then the lights grew larger, until the beams covered the sorcerers' entire bodies. The lights continued to grow brighter and brighter. So bright that it was almost blinding. There was a quick flash and the lights were instantly gone. The dark power had been drained from the sorcerers, leaving their faces drawn-in and their bodies very weak. Even too weak to speak. Their eyes seemed empty, as they just stared into space.

Glymirra's bright, blue eyes focused on them. Then she spoke, "Some of my Fae-rens will accompany all of you through the portal, which you so kindly blew-up. Then they will take you back to your old, crumbling Fortress in the Himalayan mountains. Once there, you may leave and go wherever you please."

The sorcerers, understanding the bad news, slowly looked at one another. Without powers it would be difficult for them to leave the mountain, but at least they weren't dead. Glymirra was sending them there, as she knew they would be stuck for quite a while, and she wanted peace for at least a few hundred years.

She looked to Kendar, "Please gather some soldiers and a few of the Sentinel hawks to escort them."

The Centaur nodded to his ruler and began assembling an escort of golden soldiers and Sentinels to move the sorcerers out of Wren. It only took a few mortal minutes until the large group was gone from inner Wren. Kendar watched them leave, then hurried back to the palace. He was curious to see how such an evil sorcerer as Fellon could be changed back into a non-toxic Fae-ren.

Glymirra adjusted her cape once more as she looked over all her subjects. Then she spoke, "The incantation I am about to do will require help from five hundred of my Protector Fae-rens. I will need you to form in several circles around the Cursed One. My Guardian, you will stand by me. I don't think Fellon is going anywhere."

The Fae-rens began forming the circles. The inner circle was formed first and was directly around the immobilized Fellon, his dark-hooded head hanging in defeat. The small circle was made up of twenty Fae-rens. The next circle was created around that one and was a little larger. The next group of Fae-rens made a bigger circle around that one, and it continued on until there were seven complete circles around the Cursed One.

Glymirra waited until all the Protectors where in place.

Again, she quickly scanned through the spell needed to reverse the evil curses. Looking up, the ruler waved her hand to produce a large gold ring that was three feet in diameter. As the ring floated in the air, she pointed at it and used her finger to move it until it rested directly above Fellon.

"Now I want every Fae-ren in the circles to clasp hands with the Fae-ren next to you. I will need you to concentrate on your auras and focus them into the middle of the gold ring above. Now close your eyes and direct your auras. I will perform the incantation once the ring glows a radiant yellow."

In a few short minutes the ring glowed brilliantly. Glymirra knew it was time. Nicky watched curiously, realizing he could not hear the ruler. Her mouth began to move but no sound came out.

As she continued to read the incantation, the gold ring began to vibrate. Then it shot a wide ray of the aura light down on to Fellon. The beam concentrated on him for several seconds. As soon as it touched the Cursed One, he began to scream, as if he was being tortured. The sound was very eerie and lasted for a long time. Everyone watching the transformation became terrified by the noise. It seemed to go on forever. Without warning, the ring vanished, the screaming stopped, and the hooded one collapsed. Seeing this, Glymirra knew the spell had succeeded.

She explained to the Fae-rens around Fellon. "Your auras are your soul. When combined with the power of the ancient ones in the 'Powerous,' your auras can heal a lost one. Thank you for your special help."

As magic takes a toll on the user, the exhausted Fae-rens left the circles and returned to the front of the palace to see the outcome of their auras and their leader's powerful magic.

Glymirra called to Kendar, who was watching from the corner of the palace. "Please go and bring our reborn Fae-ren to me. "

Kendar obeyed, hurrying to the dark form lying in the grass. He picked up the once powerful sorcerer. The form he was holding seemed frail and weak. As he cradled the creature in his massive arms, the dark hood fell off, revealing a red-headed Fae-ren. The crowd looked to one another, amazed by what they saw, and many even moved in closer to get a better look. None could believe their eyes. This was the most astonishing use of magic anyone had ever seen.

Nicky looked on in disbelief. He was once again in awe of such a powerful, magical ruler. No one would ever believe what the teen witnessed in the last few days. He could barely grasp the idea that a supernatural being could have such enormous mystical powers. He really felt very privileged. Tired, but privileged.

Even the Protectors were shocked by the tremendous magic they had seen. They knew their ruler was powerful, but this was beyond amazing. Many were talking amongst themselves about the supernatural experiences of the past few days.

Glymirra smiled as she looked over most of the population of Wren. A few hundred golden soldiers were still on Gaeya helping some of the displaced animals relocate to new homes, since most of their homes were destroyed by the environmental imbalance or by Evil Ones. She turned toward Nicky, smiling and nodding in thanks. Nicky smiled back. He was so thankful that the fighting was over, and the darkness was lifted.

The Grand One once more demanded everyone's attention. "I want to thank all of my Fae-rens; the Protector soldiers and also my workers. You have done an extraordinary job protecting!" Then she addressed Kendar, "I want to thank you, your Centaurs and the Sentinels. I know you lost many of your kind, and it is both very difficult and very sad, but you saved us! We could not have done it without you! I would also like to thank our mortal

Guardian, who risked his life to help both of our worlds. And last but certainly never least, a very special thanks to Brem-mer, who with help from Nicky saved your ruler and captured the evil Fellon."

"My soldiers, I will soon return you to your former Protector Fae-ren forms, and you will go back to looking after the living once more. You may be dismissed, until I am ready to transform you." Everyone started to move in different directions.

Many Fae-rens walked past Nicky and Brem-mer, whispering "Thank you", to the two heroes. Everyone was glad that soon things would return to normal.

CHAPTER 21

CACTUS FLOWER LANE

The war was over, at least for now. The Magical Beast had ended his healing and returned to the bowels of the Earth. The balance was finally restored to all of Gaeya. Mortals and animals alike came out of hiding and rejoiced.

Glymirra had Kendar take the reborn Phan-non into her palace. She would help him slowly regain his Fae-ren knowledge and keep him as her own palace helper. The Grand One looked over at Nicky and asked him to wait outside the palace entrance for her. "I will be right back. I want to check-in on my new Fae-ren."

She entered the palace sanctuary, then hurried over to see Phan-non. He was still weak but otherwise fine. Kendar had laid him on a soft area of grass and straw in a room next to the Grand One's chamber. Knowing he was alright, she left him to rest and proceeded to front of the palace. Glymirra had to keep the promise she had made to her teenage Guardian.

Nicky Kirkland stood outside the entrance of the ruler's palace. He was proud that he had been a part of saving two worlds. But now he was ready to return to his home. He missed his family and friends. The teen waited for Glymirra to reverse the spell that made him a super soldier and turn him back into an ordinary teenager once more.

The Grand One came out and walked up to Nicky. She smiled at him, saying, "You have done well, Guardian. You have far exceeded my expectations. You truly are the bravest Guardian Wren has ever had. So, now it is time for me to keep my promise and return you to the day Brin-dah and Der-rex asked for your help. But first I must turn you back to a mortal teenage boy.

"Please come and stand before me."

Nicky took a few steps forward and stood in front of the Grand One. She closed her eyes and raised her right hand over Nicky's head. Bowing his head, he heard a brief, low humming sound coming from Glymirra's mouth. Then he felt a lifting feeling all around his body. Pieces of armor flew off and disappeared. His wings went away as well. A few seconds later he felt much lighter and free of all the gold accessories. It was good to be back to normal.

Glymirra again thanked Nicky for all his help. "Please take the orb you wore. It will bring you back home. Keep it safe, and if you ever need a Fae-ren's help, use the orb."

Nicky looked around Wren one last time, trying to remember everything he saw and all the amazing creatures he had met. Brem-mer stood off to the side. He smiled and waved good-bye.

"Are you ready?" Nicky nodded, excited to finally be going home.

Just then Brin-dah and Der-rex showed up, asking the Grand One if they could accompany him home. With a nod, she waved her mighty hand, and Nicky and the two Fae-rens disappeared.

It was less than a mortal minute before the Guardian appeared on the sidewalk by his house on Cactus Flower Lane. He was dressed exactly as he had been before he left with Brin-dah and Der-rex, including his blue cap and the backpack over his shoulders. *Wow! He was home.*

He looked around. No Sentinels perched high in a tree. No crazy wind blowing everything around. No scary animals heading his way. No sorcerers hiding. It was just as he left it before he joined Brin-dah and Der-rex on their mission to return the Elka, the fourth Key of Being to Wren.

Since Nicky was unable to see the Fae-rens now, Brin-dah and Der-rex appeared as the homeless young woman and the talking brown dachshund Nicky had originally encountered five years earlier. Brin-dah gave Nicky a hug and Der-rex said "Thanks", then barked.

"Without you, we would not be here. Thank you for all your help. You really are a great Guardian and friend. Now we must go, but we will never forget you."

The two returned to their invisible Fae-ren forms. A gust of wind ruffed Nicky's hair, and he knew they were gone. He would never forget the events of the past five years. He had certainly learned a lot.

Now all the teen had to worry about was winning the State Championship at the football game tonight. It felt good to be home, but it felt even better just to be an ordinary teenager again.

CHAPTER 22

EPILOGUE

Back at Wren, the Grand One consulted the magical Reflection of Ages. A huge smile came across her large face. The blue crystal showed Nicky running for a touchdown. The crowd stood up, cheering. It was the end of the game. Nicky's School had won the Championship. Glymirra waved her hand to close the scene. All was well.